Praise for Kayleen Reusser's books:

We Fought to Win: American World War II Veterans Share Their Stories (Book 1, World War II Legacies)

This book helped to provide stories to reference when teaching about the war.
Bryan Lineberry, high school teacher and Army veteran

**

They Did It for Honor: Stories of American WWII Veterans (Book 2, World War II Legacies)

… Enough details that you'll feel you are right there in the foxhole with some of the men, or onboard a sub, or sinking a Nazi sub...

Harold Wolf, Amazon reviewer

**

We Gave Our Best: American WWII Veterans Tell Their Stories (Book 3, World War II Legacies)

This book will give the reader an intimate glimpse into the lives of dedicated men and women.

Carolyn Kramer, M.Ed. and retired teacher

**

We Defended Freedom: Adventures of World War II Veterans (Book 4, WWII Legacies)

Interviews of veterans who served in service to our country and the sacrifices they made for our freedoms make me more thankful than ever.

Chris Jones, retired teacher

1

D-Day: Soldiers, Sailors and Airmen Tell about Normandy (Book 1, World War II Insider)

I recommend this book for public libraries' WWII and local history collections as a supplement to American and World History studies.

Shana Neuenschwander, Indiana librarian

**

It Was Our War Too: Youth in the Shadows of WWII (Book 1, Witnesses of War)

School children will get a good idea of what it was like to be a child during wartime, and how it affected these individuals as adults.

Joy Kidney Neal, author of Leora's Letters

**

Captured! Stories of American WWII Prisoners of War

Reusser has told these stories in a lively narrative that includes the backgrounds of young servicemen, circumstances of each capture and difficulties they faced at the hands of their captors.

Kerry Hubartt, former publisher of the News-Sentinel (Fort Wayne, Indiana)

Battle of the Bulge: Stories from Those Who Fought and Survived

WWII Insider Series

Book 2

Kayleen Reusser

Kayleen Reusser Media

Battle of the Bulge: Stories from Those Who Fought and Survived

First published in the United States by Kayleen Reusser Media.

Printed in the United States.

www.KayleenReusser.com

ISBN 978-1-7325172-7-1

Cover illustration by Kayleen Reusser

Printed in the United States of America

Dedication

Thanks to the veterans mentioned in this book who were willing to talk with me about their battle experiences. Sadly, many of them are now deceased. Their memories and dedication kept me motivated. Without their courage, I don't know where we would be today.

Thanks to the people who assisted in my efforts to make this book as accurate as possible – James Triesler, Carolyn Kramer, Joy Neal Kidney, and Robert Kasten. Any mistakes are mine.

Thanks as always to my parents, Forace Hale and Evelyn Joan Brewer. Dad was deferred from military service for agricultural reasons, but he always respected the people who served. In later years he spent hours watching documentaries about World War II. Mom taught me to love words, spelling, and reading.

Thanks to my children -- Lindsay, Mandy, Christopher – for their support. My husband John, who is a retired Air Force airman, has served as my chauffeur, banker (he likes that part), technical wizard, research assistant, marketing consultant, encourager, videographer, photographer, calming presence and a thousand other things. He makes what I do fun.

Contents

Map of Europe

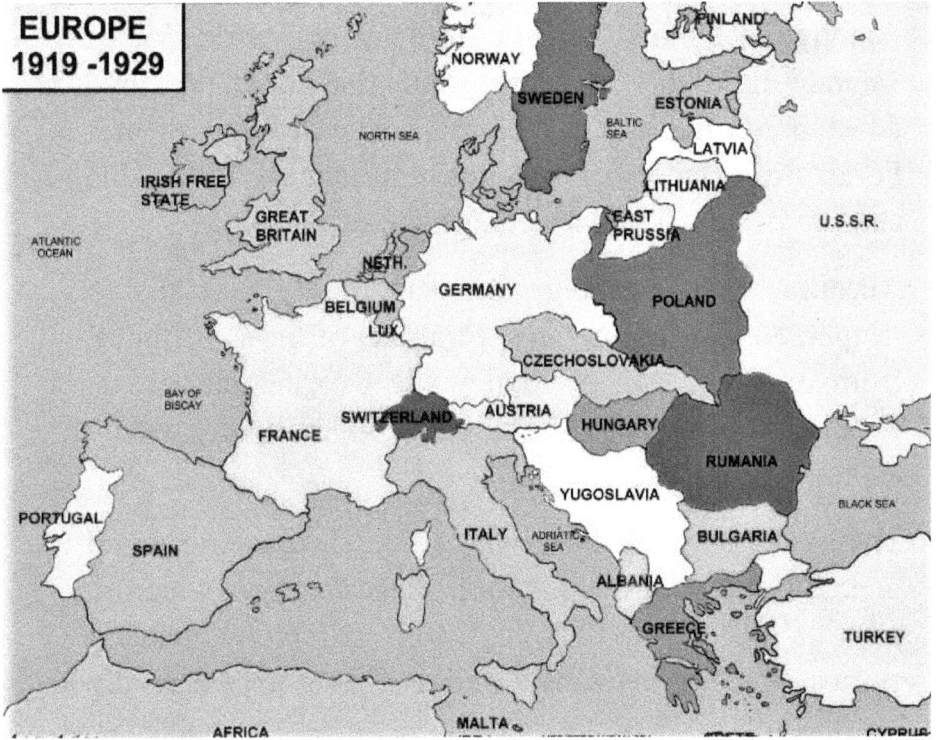

EUROPE
1919 -1929

NORWAY
SWEDEN
FINLAND
ESTONIA
BALTIC SEA
LATVIA
LITHUANIA
NORTH SEA
IRISH FREE STATE
GREAT BRITAIN
EAST PRUSSIA
U.S.S.R.
ATLANTIC OCEAN
NETH.
GERMANY
POLAND
BELGIUM
LUX.
CZECHOSLOVAKIA
BAY OF BISCAY
SWITZERLAND
AUSTRIA
HUNGARY
FRANCE
RUMANIA
YUGOSLAVIA
BLACK SEA
PORTUGAL
ITALY
ADRIATIC SEA
BULGARIA
SPAIN
ALBANIA
GREECE
TURKEY
AFRICA
MALTA
CYPRUS

1

I Wouldn't Have Wanted to Be There…
But I'm Glad They Were

Among the hundreds of stories that 260 World War II veterans have told me during the past decade are two dozen about fighting in the bitter battle in the Ardennes Forest from December 1944 through January 1945. This conflict became known as the Battle of the Bulge.

Accounts of sleeping in foxholes in sub-zero temperatures, marching in several feet of snow, suffering from frostbite, lack of food while wearing inadequate clothing, the constant fear of being killed by the enemy all amazed me.

These stories from those who selflessly gave so much make up the bulk of this book. Research was added to provide background. Note: More complete, detailed stories of many veterans mentioned here appear in my other books.

A couple of elements makes this book special. One is the memoir of an Army soldier who fought at the Battle of the Bulge.

Harold Bradley was a farmer from Elmore City, Oklahoma, when he was drafted into the Army in February 1943. He fought with the 740th Tank Battalion.

Years later, Bradley recorded his memories about serving in the Bulge. His posts provide that valued personal point of view:

"A person cannot possibly know how hellish war really is until he or she has been there. The men of the 740th Tank Battalion, most of us boys at the time, were there. We are qualified to speak."

Many photos, some never before published, are shared by veterans. Others are those I took while on a 10-day World War II Tour of Europe.

Finally, I've inserted articles from *Stars and Stripes*, the official military newspaper, printed with their exact wording and grammar during the time of the Bulge. These stories written by a variety of soldiers offer context, pathos, and even humor to this tumultuous time in America's history.

In writing this and my other books on World War II I hope to instill a greater sense of patriotism in readers. It has been distressing in recent years to witness the plummet of national pride. We are not a perfect nation. But I still believe we live in the greatest country in the world, one that offers each citizen countless freedoms and opportunities.

God bless our great country.

Prologue
The Attack
December 16, 1944

A soupy mass of fog settled in the long valley of Losheim Gap. Through the moon's dim gloom, Private John Wearly crouched under a stand of pine trees. Black rings pockmarked the landscape, painful reminders of the exploding mortar that had hit just before daybreak around the mountainous borders of Belgium and Germany. At that moment, the tranquility of the Ardennes Forest was pierced by 250,000 German troops and 600 German tanks bursting around 80,000 unsuspecting Allied troops – Canadian, British and American.

Many of the Americans had recently arrived in Europe as replacements. They had never been in battle. As they had stumbled from makeshift shelters, disoriented and terrified, their officers tried to restore order to form a counteroffensive. But the young men – some still in their teens -- were too inexperienced to hold their ground and surrendered during the hellish commotion that ensued.

Throughout the chaos, Wearly had become separated from Company M, 39th Infantry, 99th Division. During the day, he stayed hidden among the trees desperate to find his way back to the Allied front lines. Now, cold to the bone and feeling as though his stomach could eat through his insides, he trembled as the shadows seemed to shelter the enemy, intent on taking his life.

Freezing moisture had seeped into his summer-weight boots (infantry winter weight clothing had not yet arrived in the Ardennes). The discomfort made Wearly yearn to pull off his footwear and massage his cold extremities. But such an action would no doubt alert German troops of his position.

Seeking a distraction, Wearly allowed his thoughts to drift to the one place he thought of most often -- home.

An American tank destroyer pushes through enemy lines in low cloud cover.

A recent letter from his mother was full of holiday news. She had placed a wreath on the front door of their small home in Huntington, Indiana, in preparation for Christmas. A tall tree, branches heavy with handmade ornaments, stood sentry in the front room. She had also baked goodies for family and friends to snack while visiting, using what sugar rations were available. The thought of her moist cookies and cakes made Wearly's mouth water.

His mother also planned to mail him a pair of socks she was knitting. Wearly had not bothered to remind her that the deadline for mailing Christmas packages for troops had been in November. Nor did he tell her that increased troop movement and delays in the American military mail system in Europe could make receiving gifts nigh impossible.

John Wearly serves with Company M, 39th Infantry, 99th Division.

For what seemed like the millionth time Wearly wondered why he had quit his factory job back home. Assembling 20-millimeter anti-aircraft shells was a job considered vital for the war effort and it had kept him deferred from the draft.

But factory work had bored Wearly who wanted a career as a teacher. He quit his job at the factory and enrolled in education courses at Ball State University in Muncie. The change didn't go unnoticed by Uncle Sam who promptly rescinded his deferment and drafted Wearly into the United States Army.

Following completion of basic training at Camp Van Dorn at Centreville, Mississippi, Wearly was appointed to a cadre of non-commissioned officers with the 99th. At Camp Maxey near Dallas, Texas, he learned to shoot flame throwers, machine guns, bazookas (rocket launchers), and Browning rifles.

Wearly had performed well and felt equipped to face the enemy. Now, however, in the dark, dreary, and cold of the Ardennes, half a world away from everything familiar, Wearly wondered if he would live through the night.

**

At first glance the Ardennes Forest had looked enchanting to the tired Allies who arrived in early December. Charming villages set among majestic gorges and ridges made a welcome respite after a busy fall campaign of fighting the Germans.

As quiet days passed with no threat, the Allies settled in for a restful winter with lots of rest and recuperation. Some dared to believe the long war on the Western Front would end by Christmas!

American General Dwight D. Eisenhower, Supreme Allied Commander of American and British troops in

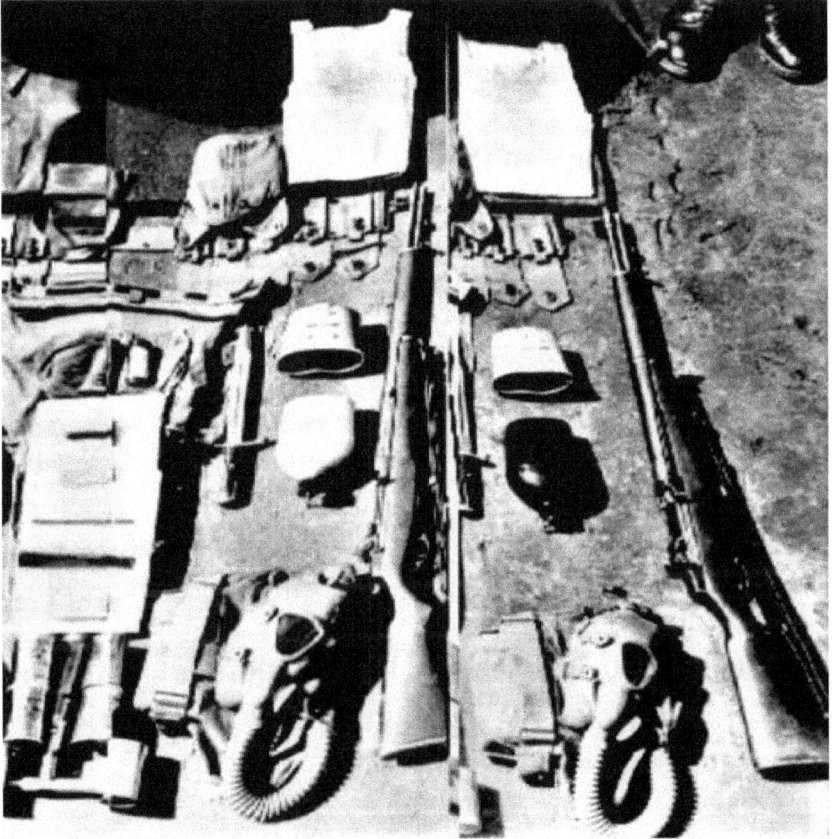

An Allied soldier's pack contains dozens of items, including canteen, olive drab G.I. blankets, and gas mask. Robert Walker.

Europe, also relaxed, believing the Germans lacked equipment for a new offensive.

Those dreams ended in the early hours of December 16th when German Chancellor Adolf Hitler ordered 30 German divisions to attack.

The six divisions of American troops, settled along their side of the border in preparation for a quiet Christmas, were ill-equipped to stand against the unexpected attack.

On a map the shape of the strike force resembled a bulky cylinder. The event that Prime Minister Winston Churchill would later call 'the world's greatest battle' would be given a name attributed to that shape: 'The Battle of the Bulge.'

**

Forcing his mind back to the present, John Wearly scrutinized the heavy fog as it drifted. He was certain the nearby hillsides contained German ski troopers dressed in white winter uniforms searching for him and other Allies.

Wearly's eyes narrowed. Staring through the dim shadows, he wondered if his mind was playing tricks as something solid took shape on the road below.

The fog cleared and the young soldier's spirits rose.

It was a jeep.

His mind raced. After waiting all day for a plan of escape, it had appeared before him. Perhaps he could dash toward the vehicle and drive off, safely dodging enemy bullets.

Then common sense halted his impulse. In which direction would he drive? After the confusion of the day, it was impossible to know the location of the fluid Allied perimeter.

Most likely the military vehicle couldn't aid his escape anyway. It had probably been abandoned due to lack of fuel. At this stage of the war gas was a precious commodity for both sides. The jeep could even be wired for explosives.

Without warning, Wearly's shoulder gripped in a painful muscle spasm. Hours of standing still had caused his shoulders to cramp and he flinched. The movement jostled pine branches around him, their soft rustling sounding like a shout in the night's silence.

Bing! Bing!

Rifle shots whistled past his ears. Wearly sprang from his hiding place. There was no time to debate a plan of escape. Struggling to maintain his balance on the treacherous, icy path, he ran down the hill toward the jeep, dismayed to see bullet holes dotting its sides. Wearly skirted the vehicle, and fled through the woods, praying his feet would lead him in the direction of the Allies – and safety.

STARS & STRIPES

16 Dec. 1944

AWOL Roundup Staged in Paris

American MPs, aided by the British and French, combed Paris yesterday, checking passes of all military personnel in a 24-hour drive to round up AWOL soldiers.

The Theater Provost Marshal said the drive was scheduled to "clean the city out" and to cut down on the increasing number of men in Paris without passes.

MPs stopped all personnel on sight, and if they did not have either a work pass, orders or a combat pass, they were taken to MP headquarters and locked up, pending investigation. To make the roundup easier for MPs, all troops stationed in Paris were restricted yesterday to their billets and the immediate area of their work.

Chapter 1: Hitler's Plan to Rule the World

Hitler's plan to divide and conquer the Allies in the Ardennes was a last-ditch effort to regain control of the war he had begun in 1939.

Long before being voted in as Chancellor of Germany in 1932 and taking office the following year, Hitler had believed the German nation could -- and should -- rule the world. While imprisoned in 1924 for a conviction of high treason, he made his thoughts known in his book *Mein Kampf*, published in 1925 (he was released after only serving nine months of a five-year term).

When German President Paul von Hindenburg died in 1934, Hitler declared himself the country's president, chancellor, and head of the army, thus making himself the absolute leader ('Fuhrer') and dictator of Germany from his headquarters in Berlin.

For six years Hitler built up his military based on the Nazi party (Nazi is abbreviation for "Nationalsozialistische Deutsche Arbeiterpartei", meaning "National Socialist German Workers' Party").

On September 1, 1939, he put his soldiers on the world's stage by invading Poland. Within a year, Hitler controlled much of Europe: Czechoslovakia, France, Greece, Luxembourg, Denmark, Norway, Netherlands, Yugoslavia, and Belgium.

Residents of each country were forced to obey the Nazi laws established by Hitler and his military. Those who disagreed were punished or killed.

The Nazis were particularly harsh to Jews, gypsies, and other groups deemed beneath their ethnic standards, murdering millions in killing centers (concentration camps) around Europe.

When news about the atrocities being committed spread to the United States, Americans were shocked at the hardships happening overseas. Still, many were reluctant to get involved in another war.

They recalled the horrific battles of WWI that occurred in France and Germany from 1914-1918. The United States had joined the war in April 1917. It concluded on November 11, 1918 – the eleventh hour of the eleventh day of the eleventh month -- with Germany's defeat. That day became known as Armistice Day. It is celebrated annually in the United States as a federal holiday referred to as Veteran's Day.

The Japanese military attack of American forces at Pearl Harbor, Hawaii, on December 7, 1941, changed most Americans' reluctance to enter the war. More than 2,400 people were killed, including 1,177 military personnel from the USS *Arizona*. The following day the United States Congress, incensed at the unwarranted attack, declared war on Japan.

Italy and Germany joined Japan as the Axis Powers fighting against the Allies: Canada, England, Australia, Soviet Union, and the United States.

**

For two years the Axis and Allied powers clashed in many places around the world, though most of the fighting took place in Europe and the Pacific. In the 1930s, as part of his battle preparations, Hitler had constructed a formidable system of obstructions along Germany's western border. Bunkers, tank traps, mines, and concrete structures extended nearly 400 miles.

The Germans referred to the line of defense as the West Wall. The Allies nicknamed it "The Siegfried Line," possibly in reference to a British World War I tune: "We're Going to Hang Out the Washing on the Siegfried Line." Hitler also created a series of defenses from France to Holland called The Atlantic Wall.

Hitler orders hundreds of miles of obstructions be constructed along the western German border.

On the Allied home fronts people worked hard to produce items needed to support their troops – crops, ammunition, planes, weapons, and more.

Despite Hitler's successful overtaking of most of Europe, his plans to expand throughout the world didn't go as expected. From September 1940 through May 1941 a blitz of German bombs dropped on British cities, causing approximately 43,000 civilian deaths in London alone. But the British people showed resilience and refused to surrender.

Then, in June 1941, Hitler ordered his troops to push into the Soviet Union. The mission called Operation Barbarossa extended several months through a bitterly cold winter, during which the Germans surrounded the city of Leningrad, cutting off food and other supplies.

St. Paul's Cathedral stands amid a fire raid in London in December 1940. National Archives.

In 1944, after a staggering siege that lasted nearly 900 days, the Red Army finally drove the Germans out. An estimated 15 million troops from both sides had engaged in battle with approximately 1,575,000 deaths.

Bent on retaliation, the Soviet Army advanced westward to Berlin in an effort to invade and take control of Nazi headquarters.

The greatest setback to Hitler's plans occurred on June 6, 1944, when the first of 156,000 Allied troops began landing on the Normandy coast of France.

Using sheer doggedness and relying on months of training, Allied soldiers secured the beaches and advanced inland, destroying enemy resistance. It was the largest amphibious invasion the world has ever known.

On June 6, 1944, American soldiers land on the coast of France under heavy German gunfire. National Archives.

Throughout the summer, the Allies fought the Germans through hedgerows and in towns and villages. With the liberation of France in August 1944, it became obvious that Hitler would be forced into a two-pronged conflict as the Soviet Army continued to march west toward Berlin.

Though everything looked hopeless for the Nazis, Hitler refused to give up. In summer 1944, he indulged his dream of world-domination by preparing for another major offensive, this time in the Ardennes. Hitler's ego was fueled by his fascination with a German legend of a battle being fought in a forest.

Hitler appointed Field Marshal Gerd von Runstedt to be in charge of the assault. The pair chose a mid-winter strike date. They believed mammoth German tanks, belching fire from their guns, would divide Allied forces, casting them in chaos. The German leaders also counted on thousands of German soldiers skulking through the mist, fog, and heavy precipitation, searching for enemy targets. Anticipated low cloud cover would force Allied planes to abandon sorties.

The resulting bedlam would enable Germany to push for Antwerp on the Belgian coast. In September 1944, Antwerp's port had been overtaken by the Allies who desperately needed it for the arrival of tons of supplies. Hitler desperately wanted to re-capture the city and disrupt the Allied supply line while obtaining fuel to keep his war machine moving.

Once the Allied supply route was severed, Hitler believed the Americans would halt their advance across Europe and seek a peace settlement. Germany could then throw its depleting strength against the Soviet Army in the East, implementing two secret weapons in development – giant rockets and jet fighters. Their use would ensure Hitler's position as a world leader.

There was one hitch to Hitler's plans.

After five years of fighting, Germany's resources were depleted. Hunger dogged soldiers and civilians alike. Young men could not be found to replenish those who had been killed, injured, or taken prisoner. To compensate the German government conscripted males ages 16 to 60 to defend the homeland, some from occupied countries that didn't speak German.

Admittedly, the challenge to replace soldiers plagued every country, including the United States. On September 16, 1940, President Franklin D. Roosevelt signed into law the Selective Training and Service Act. It required all men between the ages of 21 and 45 among the nation's 138 million citizens to register for military duty.

Following Japan's surprise attack on Pearl Harbor, Congress amended the act to require all able-bodied men ages 18 to 64 to register with their local draft board for military service for the duration of World War II plus six months after. In practice, however, only men ages 18 to 45 were drafted.

Hitler's military officers knew their country's resources were stretched. Knowing their Fuhrer didn't like criticism of his plans, they cautiously begged him to cancel the battle in the Ardennes. Hitler ignored their advice.

**

After running from the enemy for nearly an hour, John Wearly was thrilled to stumble on an Allied checkpoint.

Nearly collapsing with relief and exhaustion, his befuddled mind frantically scrambled for the password of the day for the guards.

When it became known that English-speaking German soldiers had infiltrated behind Allied lines, causing acts of sabotage, passwords became required at checkpoints.

Wearly recited the secret code and crossed the barrier, though his thoughts remained in turmoil. How many more times would he find himself in danger in the Ardennes?

**

Harold Bradley's journal:

On December 16, at 5:30 am, all hell broke loose. A six-inch blanket of white snow covered the forest floor on that dark Saturday morning. It was bitterly cold in the Ardennes. Along the 60-mile 'Ghost Front,' from the quaint community of Monschau on the German side of the Belgian border in the north to Echternach, a town in Luxembourg to the south, the Ardennes came alive.

Harold Bradley serves with the 740th Tank Battalion at the Ardennes.

At first whistles in the distance and pinpoints of fire alerted the American outpost that something unusual was

21

happening. Explosions of big German guns lit up the sky like the fourth of July.

In secrecy the German Fuhrer had amassed his powerful forces, including two Panzer Armies of 24 divisions poised and ready to strike out of the mist and fog of the Schnee Eifel, a heavily forested and protected area adjoining the Ardennes. Additional armies flanked each side to take up the slack.

My 740th Tank Battalion was ordered to deliver nine tanks to the 745th Tank Battalion. This left us with only 2,105 assault guns and three M5A1 light tanks. With that kind of equipment, we couldn't fight our way out of the mud.

STARS & STRIPES

16 DEC. 1944

CIVILIANS Asked to Let GIs Use Trains Over Holidays

So that 750,000 Christmas furloughed soldiers won't have to walk home, the Office of Defense Transportation issued its annual urgent appeal to the public to forego non-essential travel during the holidays.

The major carriers said there was only a "slim" chance for civilian reservations from east to Midwest, and Pennsylvania Railroad Officials told civilians to carry their own lunches, as servicemen have priority in diners.

Chapter 2: The Allies React
December 17, 1944

During the week following the unexpected explosion, the Allies carried out some of the most herculean troop actions in the history of warfare: the movement of 248,000 troops and 48,700 vehicles to counteract the Germans.

These quick actions vastly exceeded Hitler's estimates of Allied capabilities.

But the advancement presented logistical challenges. For each 50 miles the troops marched east, their vehicles demanded 600,000 gallons of gas. Each fighting division daily required 700 tons of food and other supplies.

To make matters worse, as Allied supplies were stored at bases in England, Hitler ordered the French channel ports of Le Havre, Boulogne, Calais, and Dunkirk to be guarded like fortresses.

The Allies would later discover to their chagrin that the Germans had still more advantages, namely in the area of communication. Movements of vast numbers of soldiers required elaborate preparations via communication. Unfortunately, Allied security in this area was lax to the point that broadcasts were made with no coded language.

By gaining access to Allied traffic control broadcasts of military police stations, the Germans were alerted to plans of troop actions.

Monitoring these transmissions and using logistic tables enabled the Germans to calculate the strength of Allied units simply based on the length of time it took a unit to pass through an area.

While blame for the Allies being caught unawares in the Ardennes arrived hard and fast, many preparations for the operation the Nazis referred to as 'Christrose', 'Autumn Mist', and 'Watch on the Rhine' had been kept top secret: night movements; towing guns via horses on straw-covered roads to muffle sounds; fighters flying low along the front line to cover the sounds of German tanks arriving at what would be the start lines.

But it could not be denied that less obscure signs of an impending battle with the Germans had occurred along the Western Front throughout fall 1944:

- Interviews with captured German prisoners revealed that Germany was preparing for an attack. The reports were considered errors in translation.
- The Sixth Panzer Army arrived in Cologne, Germany, parking their tanks in plain sight.
- By mid-December, the German military had instituted radio silence preventing Allies from listening to coded army orders and attempting to decipher them.

The Allies had not been lax throughout the fall, however. In September in the Hurtgen Forest along the German-Belgian border, approximately 120,000 troops were engaged in fierce opposition against the Germans.

"It was so cold and miserable," said Mark Flanagan of M Company, 273rd Regiment, 69th Infantry Division. "We had only summer uniforms. Lighting fires to warm us was out of the question as it would give away our positions. We didn't undress for six weeks."

Mark Flanagan of 69th Infantry Division wears a captured German helmet found in the Hurtgen Forest.

Born in Oxford, Ohio, in 1924, Flanagan was drafted and enrolled in the Army Specialized Training Program (ASTP), an educational curriculum designed to teach men to become military leaders.

At Rutgers University in New Jersey Flanagan learned engineering, foreign languages, and medicine. When the ASTP program closed a year later, Flanagan and thousands of former students were assigned to units and disembarked from the United States, arriving two weeks later at Southampton, England.

Fighting in the Hurtgen Forest deeply impressed 20-year-old Flanagan. "When enemy fire killed our unit commander, I understood the reality of war," he said.

**

Unfortunately, though the Allies fought intensely in the Hurtgen Forest, by mid-December they were forced to concede defeat.

While the Battle of Hurtgen Forest would never achieve the recognition of the Battle of the Bulge, it did claim the distinction of being the longest battle to occur on German soil during World War II. And it was costly in terms of human lives: 20,876 Allied soldiers killed; 42,893 wounded; 23,554 captured or missing.

German losses amounted to 15,652 killed; 41,600 wounded; 27,582 captured/missing.

**

Propped on the top of his half-track, Bob Staggs of 467th Engineer Battalion scanned the frozen, snow-covered countryside of the Ardennes. His tank crew had been ordered to scour the area for signs of the enemy.

The Burris High School graduate from Muncie, Indiana, wiggled his stiff fingers on the cold gun handles. Staggs usually fired two of the tank's 50-caliber machine guns, but knew he may soon need to fire all four.

In spring 1944, after completing basic training at Fort Eustis in Virginia, Staggs had sailed with the 467th to England. In Exmouth, American soldiers billeted with

Bob Staggs fought on the Normandy beaches in June 1944 before arriving at the Ardennes.

British families, as many as four per home. "Each morning we lined up in the streets of the village for roll call before beginning our training," he said.

On June 6, 1944, Staggs' unit had landed at Omaha Beach. German gun emplacements fired on LSTs (landing, ship, tank) full of troops approaching the 65-mile shore. Still, the Allies prevailed and by mid-June, the launch of the world's largest amphibious invasion allowed them to gain ground and push the Germans inland.

That summer, they liberated French villages and cities, including Paris, which had been German-occupied since 1940.

When a shot rang from a church steeple, Bob Staggs received confirmation that none in his half-track crew had been injured before ordering rounds of ammunition to be fired at the sniper.

Silence.

Staggs signaled the tank driver to move on.

**

Another group of Allied troops who scrapped through days of murderous opposition and shelling in the months leading up to the Bulge were those assigned to the 95th Infantry around Metz, France.

Daniel Boone Frazier served as a scout with the 95th. He grew up hunting on his family's farm in Kentucky, led by a

Daniel Boone Frazier learns to hunt on his family farm in Kentucky.

father who had fought in the Spanish-American war. Daniel was anxious to serve his country at war, too.

In September 1944, after completing basic training at Camp Blanding, Florida, where he qualified as a sharpshooter, Frazier disembarked with the 95th from New York Harbor for Southampton, England. The 95th sailed across the English Channel to Normandy.

In November, snow fell so thick around Metz that the troops could scarcely see enemy tanks. The weather caused problems for Frazier's sharpshooting skills. "My thumbs and forefingers were rigid with cold," he said. "I had to warm them before shooting."

By the end of the month, nothing remained of the city, nor of the German resistance, except collapsing walls and piles of rubble. The hard-fighting troops of the 95th were given the respected moniker of 'The Iron Men of Metz'.

In the Ardennes Frazier and others of the 95th would use their battlefield experience from Metz to fight the enemy.

Troops with the 95th Infantry fight so ferociously at Metz, France, that they earn the nickname, 'Iron Men of Metz.' Keith McComb.

Chapter 3: Massacre at Malmedy

Shortly after sunrise on December 17, 1944, German Colonel Joachim Peiper led First SS Panzer Division of Sepp Dietrich's Sixth Panzer Army toward the Ambleve River in eastern Belgium. After successfully storming the Ardennes a day earlier, Peiper's troops had captured an Allied gas dump at the Belgian town of Bullingen, killing dozens of American soldiers. They then advanced towards the crossroads of Baugnez near the village of Malmedy, 15 miles from the German border.

In Latin the name Malmedy translates "a malo mundarum," meaning "purifying from evil". It was assigned due to the town's history of flooding from the Warche River.

During his years of involvement with the Nazis, 30-year-old Peiper had become a ruthless leader and killer of soldiers and civilians alike. He had risen among the ranks of the German SS ("Schutzstaffel" -- German for "Protective Echelon"), a group founded in 1925. The SS served as Hitler's personal bodyguards and were the elite of the Nazi Party. None of the SS could come from Jewish bloodlines. They were considered one of the most powerful and feared organizations in all of Germany.

Around noon on the day following Hitler's push into the Ardennes, troops of Battery B, 285th Field Artillery Observation Battalion confronted Peiper's group at a junction south of Malmedy. The Americans in trucks, jeeps, and ambulances were on their way to St. Vith, 12 miles to the south with orders to join the 7th Armored Division.

It was not much of a fight. Armed with only rifles and small guns, the American convoy opened fire, but were quickly forced to surrender.

The German tank force disarmed the 130 prisoners before crowding them together in a nearby field. They then ordered their prisoners to stand, hands held high, before shooting them.

After the executions, the Germans kicked and rolled over the prone figures, checking for signs of life before resuming their journey to Baugnez.

Miraculously, 50 Americans survived the attempted assassinations. After waiting several hours to make sure the Germans didn't return, they ran to a nearby town to report the murders. Medics treated those who were injured.

"The Malmedy Massacre" would become the largest mass execution of American soldiers in the war.

When the actions of the Germans at Malmedy became known, tempers among the Allies soared. The German troops had violated rules as laid out by the Geneva Convention of 1929 in the taking of prisoners, which states that captives must at all times be treated humanely. In particular, they must be protected from acts of violence, insults and public curiosity. It was forbidden to carry out reprisals against them.

Vernon Affolder, a native of Decatur, Indiana assigned to Fifth Corps Headquarters, narrowly escaped a clash with the deadly German troops. Hours before Peiper arrived at the crossroads, Affolder and his unit had pulled out of the area.

Affolder was no stranger to death. In June 1944 he had helped load fallen soldiers on landing crafts during the Normandy invasion. But the near-miss with death at Malmedy deeply affected him. "Barely missing a confrontation with Peiper's crew was the scariest part of the war for me," he said.

**

Harold Bradley's journal:

In the villages of Neufchateau and Mortroux in the vicinity of the Meuse we were billeted in people's homes. Belgian citizens appreciated their newly-won freedom and safety provided by the presence of our troops. The GIs recognized the heartache and suffering our newfound friends had been through and valued the warmth and acceptance of the citizenry. But life for my tank battalion was about to change, drastically.

**

Elsenborn Ridge

John Wearly, re-assigned to the 99th and Second Infantry Divisions, joined his units at Elsenborn Ridge. Nicknamed by American commanders for a nearby Belgian village, the crest had been overtaken by the Germans in an effort to push through to Antwerp. But, although the Germans possessed superior armor and numbers on mainly untested soldiers, they were held in check by the Americans' defensive positions.

Still, every minute in the Ardennes seemed to present new challenges for the Allies. One morning, Wearly awakened in his foxhole to an unusual growling sound. Carefully easing his helmet-covered head over the edge, the young soldier caught his breath.

A gigantic German panzer tank rolled in his direction, turret and guns in firing position.

Scrambling on legs that wobbled like cooked noodles, Wearly thrust his body out of the dugout, running toward American 90-millimeter tank destroyers. He knew they could provide protection against the enemy.

"Every soldier in the Ardennes was scared all of the time," said Wearly. "But we knew we had to fight."

**

Facing death at Elsenborn Ridge was nothing new to Richard Willey of V Corps, 953rd Army Field Artillery Battalion. Willey, a native of Bluffton, Indiana, had enlisted in the Army after graduating from Purdue University.

In February 1944, having completed basic training at Fort Meade, Maryland, Willey boarded the *Queen Elizabeth*, a luxury liner converted to troop ship, to sail with thousands of soldiers from New York City to the British Isles.

On the moors of Scotland Willey and others from V Corps practiced shooting 155-millimeter Howitzers.

Dick Willey practices shooting cannons on the moors of Scotland before arriving in the Ardennes.

Willey's first battle experience occurred in June 1944 during the Normandy invasion. Two months later, he helped to liberate Paris. The French people, thrilled to be free after four years of occupation under German command, threw flowers at Allied soldiers who marched down the Champs-Elysees.

The warm fragrance of flowers and summer scenes were far from Willey's mind as he braved stark weather at Elsenborn. "One time I crawled inside a pillbox for protection from the record-low temperatures," he said. "It was like a metal igloo with no air so I went back outside."

STARS & STRIPES

18 Dec. 1944

Gramp, Gramp, the Boys are Marching

WITH THE FIFTH INF. DIV., GERMANY

In what was probably the most unorthodox engagement in military annuals, two dozen septuagenarian selectees put on a 150 min exhibition which looked more like something from an Olson and Johnson show than a last-ditch battle. Ten of the Volkssturmers bit the dust, one shot himself in the leg, and nine others threw down their antique French carbines and yelled "kamarac." (May have been the word 'kamerad', which translated in German means 'comrade'.)

One of the wrinkled oldsters, questioned about the formation of the unit, training and size, said there were 500 men in the Metz unit but when the call to arms came, 476 were AWOL.

Harold Bradley's journal:

Orders were received from First U.S. Army Headquarters that we were to move to the ordnance vehicle depot at Sprimont, Belgium. There we would equip ourselves with whatever combat vehicles were available and advance to Aywaille. On the Ambleve River, a few miles southwest of Spa, we would take up defensive positions and slow the deadly German thrust.

Company "C" commanded by Captain James D. Berry moved out in GI trucks. We troops wondered about the location of the prized Sherman tanks we had trained on. Their 75-millimeter cannons could tear out the side of a building. A Sherman's 30-caliber machine guns could chop a sniper to splinters.

The equipment was nowhere to be found.

Panic spread up and down the front. This was no way to go into battle. How could we fight a powerful enemy that crushed everything in its way without tanks?

We arrived at the ordnance depot to grab what armor we could find. Colonel Rubel took off with his liaison officer for Aywaille to report on the Ambleve, then scouted the area to be defended.

He learned an armored task force was 12 miles off, coming our way. As we still did not have any fighting machines, we desperately tried to make something to fight in from leftover tanks at the ordnance depot at Sprimont.

The atmosphere was bedlam. There were perhaps 25 tanks of different types, including three M4 Sherman's medium tanks in which we had trained. They all had parts destroyed or missing.

What was left in the pile ranged from M5 and M24 light tanks to old M7 and open-topped M10 assault gun motor carriage and even a M36 tank destroyer with a high velocity 90-mm gun.

Working throughout the night, we took parts from one vehicle and put them on others. It was demoralizing, backbreaking, heart-wrenching work. For a while it looked like there was no light at the end of the tunnel.

By the next morning we had put together what barely looked like a tank company. Captain Berry shouted, "All right, let's move 'em out!"

Our untested young tankers headed for Remouchamps in the Ambleve Valley.

The ragtag column of tanks clattered up to the command post. After being briefed, we were ordered into the attack. The ground steadied under our feet.

STARS & STRIPES

18 Dec. 1944
*Paris Joints Still Jumping
Despite the Ban on Dancing*

Despite the official ban, dancing in Paris nightclubs and cabarets flourished over the weekend, with dance floors open to all comers.

Troops with pass and GIs stationed in the French capital, having read that the police had outlawed dancing in public places, made the rounds and found nightspots in full swing.

Everyone else was a little confused, too.

Cabaret proprietors in Montmartre, hub of Paris nightlife, said they didn't know anything about any injunction against dancing. They "thought" that the rule applied only to nightclubs on the Champs-Elysees.

December 19, 1944

When the 106th Infantry Division dug in the 65-mile distance between Monschau, Germany, and Echternach, Luxembourg, they created a salient in the German bulge. However, their impact was diminished when 7,000 Allied troops, clothed in light-weight uniforms, surrendered. Possibly they preferred the possibility of survival inside a German prison over enduring the frigid wilderness of the Ardennes.

"I saw soldiers freeze to death," said Virgil Bixler of the 80th Division, 905th Field Artillery. Bixler was married and farming near Geneva, Indiana, when drafted in 1942. By the time he boarded the *Queen Mary*, bound for Europe, his wife, Garnett, was expecting the couple's first child.

It was a challenge for Bixler to leave his pregnant wife, but he did not turn back. "I was trained and ready to fight," he said. A bright spot occurred for

Virgil Bixler's son is born while he fights in Europe.

Bixler when he received a letter from home several months

later -- his wife had delivered a son. "I kept our son's photograph close to me as I fought," he said.

STARS & STRIPES

19 Dec. 1944

Patrol Dons Long Johns For Use As Snow Suits

WITH SECOND INF. DIV., Inside the Siegfried Line –

Ingenious Yanks pulled out their long winter underwear and used them for camouflage suits when snow caught troops without proper clothing.

"We painted our helmets white and put drawers and tops over our other clothing," Cpl. John K. Smith, of Louisville, explained. "It worked pretty good." Camouflage suits were later issued and the underwear returned to its accustomed use.

In his Order of the Day General Eisenhower addressed soldiers throughout the Ardennes:

"The enemy is making his supreme effort to break out of the desperate plight into which you forced him by your brilliant victories of the summer and fall.

He is fighting savagely to take back all you have won and using every treacherous trick to deceive and kill you.

He is gambling everything but already in this battle your gallantry has done much to fell his plans.

In the face of your proven bravery and fortitude he will completely fail. But we cannot be content with his mere repulse.

By rushing from his fixed defenses, the enemy may give us the chance to turn his great gamble into his worst defeat.

So I call upon every man of all of the allies to rise now to new heights of courage, resolution and effort. Let everyone hold before him a single thought to destroy the enemy on the ground, in the air, everywhere destroy him.

United in this determination and with unshakable faith in the cause for which we fight, we will with God's help go forward to our greatest victory.

**

Foxholes

During the bitterly cold weeks of fighting in the Ardennes Forest, soldiers considered themselves lucky to find shelter. While abandoned buildings and barns offered optimum choices of protection from the enemy and severe weather, more often troops were forced to seek refuge beneath the earth's surface in foxholes.

Most soldiers learned about foxholes long before arriving in Europe. During basic training, Dennis Butler, a student at Manchester University in Indiana (then Manchester College), practiced digging foxholes with his collapsible entrenching tool (shovel).

A soldier practices digging foxholes during training.

A typical foxhole, measuring approximately five-by-five feet with a depth of two feet, could accommodate two soldiers.

Foxholes were far from perfect, but crucial as a way for troops to take cover from machine gun fire, as well as shrapnel from artillery shells. Infantry men were targeted by snipers only when they moved out of foxholes.

Soldiers live in tents in basic training and the Ardennes. Dennis Butler.

Butler, assigned to General George S. Patton's Third Army, 76th division, Company G weapons platoon, had sailed to England in late 1944 on the USS *Sea Owl*, a converted cargo ship. "It looked like a bathtub and I was seasick for three days," he said.

After crossing the English Channel to LeHavre, France, Company G rode in unheated 40-and-8 train cars to Luxembourg. The term '40-and-8' refers to the practice during WWI of loading railroad cars with 40 men or eight horses. Like their equine patriots, Butler and the other soldiers slept on straw.

In the Ardennes Butler grew to appreciate his foxhole training. "One time my unit was hunkered down for three days while shells flew over us," he said. "Those holes in the ground saved our lives."

Once, when Max Whiteleather, assigned to the 820th Engineer Aviation Battalion, Co. A, raised his helmeted head during a battle to check his surroundings, a shell whizzed past his head.

Max Whiteleather works on the Pennsylvania Railroad prior to the war.

He quickly ducked out of sight. "I still have ringing in my ears from that bullet," he said.

Born in 1920 in Elkhart, Indiana, Whiteleather worked on the Pennsylvania railroad before being drafted in 1942. The 820th built air strips and pontoon bridges for troops to cross rivers.

Whiteleather gained his first battlefield experience at Omaha Beach in June 1944. The approach to shore was rough as troops clambered over the sides of ships using rope nets. Enemy bullets pinged the water as they frantically approached the French shore. The bodies of Allied soldiers lay in the water and on the ground by the time they dug in behind hedgerows.

**

Sometimes foxholes in the Ardennes were unavailable. After participating with thousands of other soldiers in the Tennessee Maneuvers (exercises simulating battle conditions), Millard Schwartz, a native of Jay County in Indiana and assigned to the 94th Division, sailed in July 1944 from New York to Scotland.

The troops moved to France and months later, became part of the Battle of the Bulge. "That area of Europe had recorded subzero temperatures and much snowfall," said Schwartz.

"We slept in blankets that stuck to the ice-covered ground. We couldn't put up a pup tent or dig foxholes because the ground was frozen."

**

Millard Schwartz prepares for battle at the Tennessee Maneuvers.

**

Harold Bradley's journal:

The 30th Infantry Division needed help before it was completely overrun so we were assigned to its 119th Infantry Regiment. Third Platoon (mine) commanded by Lieutenant Charles Powers was to spearhead the attack with first and second platoons following.

Our column of tanks slowed to a crawl as we moved toward the front. A chilling rain-drenched fog and long lines of battle-scarred troops worked their way wearily

50

to the rear. They said we were crazy to go up there as it was 'a slaughter and bloodbath.'

As we rolled forward, another American tank company fell back, withdrawing from the fight due to low ammo and fuel.

When our column reached the front, the 119th began to filter into the forest abreast of our tanks. Lt. Powers and his loader stood heads out of their turret hatches when they spotted a German tank.

Jack Ashby, Powers' gunner, fired a round that hit and ricocheted downward – a lucky strike considering the Panzer's thick armor. The German tank exploded and burst into flames.

Minutes later, Powers spotted another tank. Again Ashby got off the first shot. This time the shot ricocheted up and spun away. When Ashby's gun jammed, Powers assigned his Number 2 tank commanded by Staff Sergeant Charlie W. Loopey to move up.

Loopey and his crew were in an M36 tank destroyer with a 90-mm gun. As the German tank moved forward to get into position to shoot, Loopey told his gunner to fire.

After several rounds, they blew up the tank. When Powers' crew faced a third Panzer tank across the road, Ashby's first shot blasted the muzzle brake of the German's cannon. Ashby continued to fire as the tank backed away, finally setting it on fire. Together with the 119th Infantry's 1st Battalion, we regained more than

1,000 yards of bitterly contested front given up earlier that day. Afterward, we slept as good as we could in our tanks.

Allied troops fight the Germans and weather in the Ardennes. Beresford Clarke.

STARS & STRIPES

19 Dec. 1944

Last of Three Sons Sent Back Home

WITH THE SECOND INFANTRY DIVISION, Germany

The long road home begins now for Pfc. George T. Shelton, of Channelview, Tex., who has been in action with the Ninth Inf. Div. since D plus 2.

Shelton, 23, a BAR man, was ordered home by the War Department because he is the last of three sons left in his family. He doesn't know how his two brothers met death.

The oldest, Sherrill, was in the Engineers and the youngest, George, was in the 38th Infantry.

Shelton was wounded in the leg by shrapnel at St. Germaine d'Elle, France, in July, evacuated to England, and rejoined his outfit in September.

"I would rather stay here," he said, "and have my brothers back."

Chapter 4: Securing Bastogne
December 20, 1944

Stalled by a powerful Allied buildup north of the Bulge, the Germans switched their main thrust to the central Ardennes. General Hasso von Manteuffel's Fifth Panzer Army attacked a hodge-podge of American forces defending vital crossroads at St. Vith, a key road junction in eastern Belgium.

In 1944, von Manteuffel, a WWI veteran promoted to General of the Panzer Troops, was given command of the Fifth Panzer Army on the Western Front. He had the unenviable task of reaching the Meuse River and taking Brussels and Antwerp back from the Americans.

With the Allies thwarting the Fifth Panzers, the village of Bastogne, 34 miles southwest of St. Vith, became a highly sought-after location.

Seven roads radiated from Bastogne's center, making the village the hub of the southern Ardennes road network. Whoever controlled the small Belgian market town would be assured of rapid ease of movement for tanks, artillery and troops.

Under the leadership of General Anthony McAuliffe, the United States 101st Airborne Division was called upon to secure the area. Approximately 15,000 soldiers and their vehicles made a valiant effort on icy roads to arrive before the enemy. Though freezing wind slashed through the clothing of troopers riding in open-bed vehicles, the first trucks slid into the village hours before German soldiers of the 47th Panzer Corps surrounded the town.

The 82nd Airborne chooses Le Chateau Naveau de Bra-sur-Lienne as its command post during the Bulge. Photo by author.

Over the next several days Allied troops endured constant bombardment from German units led by General Heinrich Freiherr von Luttwitz. Low cloud cover and ground fog continued, prevented Allied planes from bombing the enemy and dropping badly-needed supplies -- weapons, ammunition, overshoes, blankets, and food.

As days passed with no replacements of ammunition, the 101st Airborne had no choice but to take on a defensive position -- firing only when absolutely necessary.

The weather presented an additional concern. American M1 rifles fired by infantry soldiers were prone to malfunction in extremely cold conditions. This was due to the congealing of lubricants used to clean the guns. When a cold weapon was fired, the action did not cycle, forcing the soldier to manually cycle the operating rod which cycled the bolt. After a few rounds, the action warmed and the gun cycled normally. To ensure mechanisms on their rifles did not freeze, the troops regularly cycled the actions.

STARS & STRIPES

20 Dec. 1944

5 Packs for All is Butt Ration for Next Week

Com Z headquarters announced yesterday that the cigarette ration next week for all soldiers supplied by PXs would be five packs, providing "a uniform ration for all personnel in the ETO."

The announcement added: "When stocks have reached the necessary level the normal ration of seven packs will be resumed."

When Eisenhower heard about the desperate situation of the beleaguered troops at Bastogne, he ordered Patton and his Third Army to relieve them as soon as possible.

A soldier transports General George S. Patton (far right) and American Secretary of War Henry Stimson (center) in a jeep in Europe. Keith McComb.

Patton was a native of California, an expert horseman, and consummate soldier. Known for dressing in shiny cavalry boots with ivory-handled revolvers riding on each hip, he had led Allied troops earlier in the war in fighting the Germans in North Africa and the Mediterranean.

Patton never doubted his 80,000 ground troops, tanks, and bulldozers could overtake and conquer Hitler's troops in the Ardennes.

When Patton received the order from Eisenhower to aid the beleaguered troops at Bastogne, the Third Army was 120 miles to the south. Despite horrendous travel conditions, Patton immediately turned his troops and vehicles with supplies northward.

That first day the troops drove in trucks with hatches open, ready to fire. They traveled more than half of the distance through a snowstorm, barely stopping to sleep.

Daniel Frazier rode in back of one of the uncovered trucks. "That was the coldest I have ever been in my life," he said.

Although cloudy weather prevented the Allies from dropping supplies, it may have ultimately helped Patton's troops on their trek to Bastogne. German planes that otherwise would have had the opportunity to slaughter the long, bumper-to-bumper troop movements were also grounded.

Keith McComb's Christmas card reflecting his military involvement during the war.

58

Feeding the Troops

Receiving the right amount of nutritious food was vital for Allied troops on the battlefield. Thanks to government support and new technology, those soldiers during World War II were offered better rations than in previous wars, though some may have argued the point.

Scientists developed high-calorie, non-perishable foods that were issued in boxed and canned kits called 'C' rations. These packages were designed to be portable and at least minimally tasty. The rations contained a variety of meat products, including hash, meat stew with vegetables or beans, chopped ham, egg, potato, ham and beans, and chicken.

American infantry soldiers receive meal rations in Belgium, January 1945. National Archives.

Miscellaneous food items consisted of compressed cereal, biscuits, peanuts, raisins, powdered coffee drink, sugar, powdered orange drink, hard candies, jam or cocoa powdered drink. A kit may also contain toilet paper, gum, can-opener, water-purifying tablets, salt, wooden spoon, cigarettes, and matches.

Other food supplements called 'K' rations were packaged in color-coded boxes – brown/ breakfast; red/ lunch; blue/ supper. Wooden cases used to package 'K' rations were used as firewood or as lining for foxholes.

Food often had to be eaten cold, as a fire could attract enemy attention. Troops learned alternative means of

Troops eat rations whenever and wherever possible -- in this case, atop a box. Beresford Clarke.

heating food -- placing cans on warm truck motors or in garbage cans filled with hot water.

In the central area of the Ardennes, paratroopers of the 101st Airborne and supporting Allied units established a 16-mile perimeter. Three panzer divisions bypassed Bastogne, while Von Manteuffel's spearhead stormed toward the Meuse River.

While fighting in the Ardennes, Beresford Clarke turns 21 years old.

In its advance toward Bastogne, the Third Army counterattacked the south side of the Bulge. The assault gained them seven miles over treacherous fields and icy roads.

The Fifth Panzer Army took St. Vith, but at St. Lo members of Patton's 26th Yankee Division beat off strong resistance.

On that day, while fighting house-to-house, blowing holes in walls, and engaging in firefights, Private First Class Beresford Clarke, a mechanical engineering student from Purdue University, harbored a secret.

He turned 21 years old.

Clarke kept news of his birthday to himself. "General Patton had given his 'Blood and Guts' speech to us recruits during boot camp," he said. "He stressed to us the seriousness of war. When he was done, we knew we were to be engaged in a deadly game. He would not tolerate distractions in battle."

As it turned out, Beresford Clarke's birthday was not without blessings. At noon his platoon approached a group of peasants standing by the road. The farmers offered to ladle hot cabbage soup into the soldiers' canteen cups. "I never tasted anything so good," said Clarke. He was still thinking about the soup that night as he and his tent mate pitched their shelter halves (tent) in a foot of snow.

**

STARS & STRIPES 25 Dec. 1944

Puppy Tent

They couldn't have picked a better name of pup-tents, according to Pfc. Isadore Schwartz, of Philadelphia, PA., and Pvt. Frank B. Wilson, of Boston. The two were sitting under their hunk of canvas at a replacement depot, griping about the mud and rain when they heard a dog whining outside.

They let her in, bedded her down on a blanket, and continued griping. Sometimes later they heard more whining. Their guest had given birth to a litter of seven pups.

Chapter 5: The Ghost Front

In Fall 1944, Division Commander General John Leonard, desiring to give his men of the Ninth Armored Division a feel for combat, obtained permission for them to relieve other troops on the front line. For two months the Ninth learned to fight strategically. In fact, so many times did the Germans report that they had destroyed the Ninth, only to have it pop up again, that the American soldiers were given the nickname, "Phantom Division".

To further cement the impression of an ethereal presence the Ninth fought in a place of the Ardennes so filled with fog that the region was nicknamed "Ghost Front."

The idea of a ghostly aura had been attached to the troops earlier upon sailing across the Atlantic on the *Queen Mary*, the largest and most luxurious ocean liner in the world. During the war, the *Queen,* owned by the Cunard Steamship Company line, had been converted for military use as a troop ship, capable of carrying as many troops as possible—up to 16,000.

The ship's body and windows were painted a drab gray with hopes she would be less noticeable to U-boats in the Atlantic, thus earning the nickname "The Gray Ghost".

In reality, the ship's appearance was possibly not as effective in eluding the enemy as her speed -- she could travel at 30 knots. The Atlantic Ocean was filled with German U-boats, looking for quarry. A German submarine needed 20 minutes to sight a torpedo. The *Queen* sailed on a zig-zag course, switching direction every 15 minutes. As she was thought to be able to escape danger, the *Queen* usually sailed without escort.

**

In early fall 1944 Tech. Sergeant Ray Boyer from Virginia, sailed across the Atlantic Ocean on the *Queen Mary*. Assigned to the Ninth Armored Division, Co. A, Second Tank Battalion, CCR, Boyer and his unit landed in Scotland before traveling to England. From there they sailed across the English Channel to France. In October, the Ninth entered the Ardennes Forest between Belgium and Luxembourg.

After Hitler drove his troops between American and British units, the three combat commands of the Ninth Armored Division -- CCA, CCB, CCR (Reserve) -- were attached to major commands. The CCA was initially in the south at Beaufort, Luxembourg, then at Bastogne with the Fourth Armored Division.

The CCB fought in the north to delay the German capture of St. Vith.

The CCR fought in the middle, aiding the defense of Bastogne. Their instructions were to hold the roadblocks at all costs. It didn't take long for Boyer to realize the Allies were fighting a deadly battle, not only with the enemy, but natural elements. Believing he would most likely still be fighting through the winter, Boyer wrote to his family, asking them to send arctic boot liners. He later attributed this protection for saving his feet.

Along with the 28th Infantry Division and CCB of the 10th Armored, the CCR absorbed the first shock of the German attack. Their delay tactics stalled the enemy for days, resulting in losses to the Germans of valuable time, terrain, and combat power.

By stopping German attacks, the Ninth gave the 101st and 82nd Airborne Divisions time to arrive and lift the siege of Bastogne. They also saved much of Luxembourg from another German invasion.

Ray Boyer of the Ninth Armored Division trains at Camp Ibis in California before leaving for Europe. Carolyn Kramer

**

Harold Bradley's journal:

When our attack bogged down, we lost three tanks. We had been trying to call in an air strike, but the strike was cancelled. Same old story -- poor visibility. Casualties ran high. Infantry Battalion alone lost nearly 200 men.

Chapter 6: Nuts!
December 22, 1944

When two German soldiers approached the Allied lines in Bastogne waving a white flag, the besieged troops received a reprieve from the barrage of shelling -- but it was short-lived.

The Germans carried a message from General Heinrich von Luttwitz to General Anthony McAuliffe– a demand that the Allies surrender. If they refused, the Germans would attack.

Luttwitz had accurately assessed the situation. The 101st was dreadfully ill-equipped to continue withstanding the ongoing assault. Gray clouds continued to dominate the skies, forcing Allied flight crews to stay grounded. The Germans confidently believed the Allies' resolve had weakened them enough to give up.

It appeared McAuliffe had a tough decision to make. McAuliffe knew his soldiers were cold, hungry and outnumbered approximately five to one.

But McAuliffe was a resolute soldier. The 46-year-old had grown up in Washington D.C. and graduated from West Point Military Academy. During the war, he led the 101st in parachuting into Normandy on D-Day and landed in a glider as a part of Operation Market Garden in Holland.

In response to the German ultimatum to surrender McAuliffe uttered a one-word reply: "Nuts!"

According to reports recorded about the confrontation, the Germans were initially confused by the terse response. Then, upon deducing its meaning, an infuriated von Luttwitz ordered an attack on the Allies that included the Luftwaffe (German Air Force). The Allies managed to ward off the enemy.

But the question remained — how much longer could they hold on?

STARS & STRIPES

24 Dec. 1944

Casual GIs Earned This Meal

This is Pfc. Mike L. Volpe's story of how his squad in L Co., 320th Inf. of the 35th Inf. Div. took time out from dinner to capture another German town.

"Our squad took a town and five of us put four chickens on the stove to cook. We had potatoes and peas, too. We had a good meal cooking and the order came down for our platoon to send some men to take another town.

"So we took the chickens and the pot and took off across the field. Our sergeant told us if we ran into any Jerries we would have enough fire to cook them.

We crossed water up to our waist but we still carried the chickens. Luck was with us. We took the town without any trouble and then finished cooking our chickens. What a meal it was. Worth taking the chickens!"

Harold Bradley's journal:

That night Jerry sent over a good many transport planes. We feared they were dropping paratroopers. Instead, they dropped ammunition, fuel and rations for Colonel von Peiper's German task force, to whom we had given a beating. Some of the fuel and ammo fell in our laps so the German task force came up a little short. During our fighting for the Belgian towns of Spa, Stoumont and La Gleize, we counted over 175 vehicles knocked out. We lost six tanks and ten men were wounded. No one was killed.

One of the best fighting infantry divisions we were attached to was the 82nd Airborne. They worked well with us wherever we fought together.

**

STARS & STRIPES

"Dear mom: Cancel that request of mine for homemade candy and send me more shells for Christmas. D ration chocolate will substitute for candy but nothing can take the place of more shells."

71

Fighting From the Air

Each day during the siege at Bastogne, First Lieutenant Don Shady, co-pilot with the 78th Troop Carrier Squadron, 435th Troop Carrier Command, scanned the skies, hoping for a break in the low cloud cover.

The pre-med major from Indiana University had enlisted in the Army Air Corps in December 1942, training in courses of math, geography, Morse code, weather, and aircraft identification while flying PT-19s and AT-7s.

Don Shady drops much-needed supplies to troops in the Ardennes.

In January 1944, Shady was sent to Welford Park, England, an American military site 60 miles west of London. For months he piloted cargo planes, pulled gliders, hauled troops and freight, until dropping paratroopers over occupied Holland as part of Operation Market Garden in September 1944.

Two days before Christmas, the week-long spell of bad weather finally abated. Control towers from England to Belgium sent every Allied plane that could fly -- more than 5,000 – to the defenders at Bastogne.

Flight crews loaded their C-47s with chute drops of 144 tons of supplies. The re-supply continued the next day with 100 tons.

Though the Germans fired heavy flak and many planes were shot down, Allied aircrews refused to use evasive action, knowing the food, medical, and ammunition supplies had to be dropped on target. "We hated that low cloud cover prevented us from taking in supplies early," said Shady, "but we made up for it."

Supplies were not the only items the pilots delivered. From December 23-27, the Ninth Air Force dropped a daily average of nearly 550 tons of bombs on German troops, vehicles, and lines of communication. Allied bombers from the Eighth Air Force shattered roads, railroads, and bridges.

German supply convoys moving up from the rear received a pounding by massive armadas. Their tanks and infantry columns in the Ardennes, which had spent a week using open roads without risk, were trounced by Allied dive bombers whose planes also destroyed bridges and attacked huge German tanks which Hitler had used to block roads.

In another instance Allied ground troops, trying to fight off German Tiger tanks and planes firing 50-caliber machine guns, called for assistance. Within minutes two P-47's from the Ninth Tactical Air Force strafed the tanks.

The P-47s were equipped with eight 50-caliber machine guns synchronized to fire 400 yards in front of the plane.

When one plane began to smoke, Allied troops watched in horror as it rolled over on its back. The pilot bailed out with his chute, and a ground unit rushed to pick him up. Thankfully, he was uninjured.

By this time the German Air Force, which at the beginning of the war had dominated the skies, was nearly done.

The primary reason -- an insufficient supply of air fuel.

An American pilot prepares his bird for another mission in Europe. Keith McComb.

The Allies utilize P-47 Thunderbolts to fight the enemy in Europe. Jim Fall.

When British General Bernard Montgomery reported to Eisenhower of an acute shortage of infantry in the First and Ninth Armies, he did not underestimate the situation. In V Corps alone there was a deficit of 7,000 riflemen. Afraid of renewed German attacks to the north, Montgomery convinced Eisenhower to wait until January 2 to see if the Germans would attack.

In the southern Ardennes Patton's troops did not hold back, counterattacking within 12 miles of Bastogne before fierce resistance and thick minefields slowed the advance.

December 24, 1944

Despite the stalwart determination of Patton's soldiers and paratroopers to arrive at Bastogne, tank units of the Fifth Panzer Army infiltrated the village streets first, killing and wounding approximately 3,500 men of the 101st.

Although they pressed on, inclement weather prevented significant Allied progress of the First and Third armies. Weary and bloodied, they managed to make small gains in the Rohr River Valley and the Saarland.

In desperation Patton approached Father James Hugh O'Neill, an American Roman Catholic chaplain who had served in the Philippine Islands. Patton had an unusual request for the minister: Ask God to send better weather.

O'Neill complied. His prayer was printed and distributed to unit members:

"Almighty and most merciful Father, we humbly beseech Thee, of Thy great goodness, to restrain these immoderate rains with which we have had to contend. Grant us fair weather for battle. Graciously hearken to us as soldiers who call upon Thee that, armed with Thy power, we may advance from victory to victory and crush the oppression and wickedness of our enemies, and establish Thy justice among men and nations. Amen."

According to reports, the weather improved soon after. In deep gratitude Patton awarded O'Neill a Bronze Star Medal.

**

As the Second Panzer Division advanced toward Antwerp, the tenacity of the Allies and their ability to adapt in battle shone. Heavy attacks were made on German air fields to cut down their air support. Though the Luftwaffe was now far from being the superior air force as it had been at the beginning of the war, it still averaged 600 daily sorties from December 23-26. This was the heaviest German air activity since Normandy.

Von Rundstedt knew his troops could not reach the Meuse River. However, when the Commander-in-Chief in the West advised Hitler that the Germans should go on the defensive, the Fuhrer refused.

Rundstedt was not the only one of Hitler's military leaders who tried to get the Fuhrer to change his mind about the Ardennes offensive. Heinz Guderian, Hitler's Chief of Staff of the Army, pleaded with Hitler to give reserve troops to the Eastern Front to fight in the Soviet Union. Again, Hitler refused, throwing more reserves into the fight in the Ardennes.

**

When Bob Foster's captain handed him a Browning Automatic Rifle (BAR), Foster didn't question the duty. The BAR was a .30-caliber light machine gun with 20-round magazine that the American infantry used against the enemy. Foster knew the likelihood of surviving with the BAR was minimal. It offered little protection from German tanks firing 88-millimeter shells -- and his unit's first BAR man had been killed.

But, during WWI, Foster's father had served in the French Signal Corps. Bob Foster believed it was his duty as well to give his all in service to his country and enlisted in the Army in 1942. At their home in Bluffton, Indiana, Bob told his wife Phyllis, "I have to go and fight."

After completing basic training at Aberdeen Proving Ground in Maryland, Foster trained as a tank mechanic with the 84th Infantry Division Railsplitters, Company A, 333rd Regiment. In summer 1944, he sailed to Europe where, six months later, he was involved in the brutal conflict of the Ardennes.

When enemy fire caught his captain in the leg, Foster pressed his hand against the officer's wound to staunch the flow. Sadly, it was a mortal wound and the officer died.

Foster had ignored injuries to his knee and head and collapsed. Medics and litter bearers rushed him to an aid station and Foster was eventually transferred to hospitals in Paris and England.

STARS & STRIPES
December 24, 1944
By Andy Rooney

Turkey Plentiful Back Home – If the Butcher is Your Pal
New York, Dec. 23 –

You have to "know" the butcher to get a turkey but most housewives know one, and anyone in the United States who is really making an effort, will have a turkey for Christmas.

There is no shortage in the fixings which go with the big bird, and even delicacies like figs, dates, and avocados are plentiful. There seems to be no shortage of Christmas candy of the traditional striped variety but the well known brands of bars are not easily available. Bars like "Whatzitts, Ohyoukids, and GI Joe" are in great demand.

Chapter 7: Treating the Wounded

Medics in the Ardennes were kept busy -- seven out of 10 deaths involved infantry soldiers, or 'ground pounders.'

Bob Batchelder of Fort Wayne, Indiana, served as a litter bearer with the 457th Army Medical Collecting Company. His mission was to get injured and dead bodies off the field – often near the front lines -- on litters (stretchers) as quickly and safely as possible.

Batchelder had gained experience in battle during the landing on Omaha Beach on June 6, 1944, as part of the D-Day invasion. Batchelder's division supported the 82nd Airborne Division. "I crawled down the side of our landing craft with medical supplies into the cold water while guns strafed the water around us," he said. "Thankfully, I knew how to swim."

Bob Batchelder serves as a medic at D-Day and the Bulge.

As paratroopers, parachute artillery elements, and other troops landed for the assault on the shores of Normandy, Batchelder assisted medical personnel in tents that served as temporary field hospitals. Six months later, he assisted injured troops calling for help from foxholes in the Bulge.

Gene Valentine treats casualties on the battle-field with a new drug -- penicillin.

Morphine as a method of treatment had been used earlier in the war. However, at a field hospital in Bastogne Gene Valentine was thrilled to use a new miracle drug called penicillin. "It was thought to be a cure-all by medics," he said.

Born in Liberty Center, Indiana, in 1924, Valentine was drafted into the Army in 1943. He attended basic training at a hospital in Chicago before riding a train to Vancouver where he trained in another hospital as a medical technician. "All of our patients were soldiers," he said.

Penicillin's amazing properties for healing offered another benefit as a distraction to the staff. "The merciless sounds of war around us never stopped," added Valentine. "We constantly wondered if we would make it through the day. Knowing we were doing some good helped us get through it."

**

James 'Andy' Anderson assigned to the 94th Medical Gas Treatment Battalion, Third Army, and other medics differed from regular soldiers in two significant ways. One was that they didn't carry weapons on the battlefield. Instead, they relied on armed Allied soldiers for protection while treating the wounded with bandages, iodine, and sulpha packets.

Second, medics wore white armbands, each with a Red Cross over the sleeve. According to Rules of the 1929 Geneva Convention, military medical personnel were to be protected from enemy fire. The armbands were thought to help with identification in the heat of battle.

Anderson, who like many soldiers had fought on the beaches of Normandy six months earlier, found the Belgian countryside around Bastogne in December 1944 different. "Instead of treating the wounded in sand, I worked in frigid temperatures that made my hands ache," he said.

STARS & STRIPES
"Army Weighs Combat Money for the Medics"
WASHINGTON, Dec.15

-- The War Department is studying possible additional recognition for Medical Corps enlisted personnel serving with combat units comparable to combat insignia and extra pay for infantrymen, Secretary of War Stimson said today.

His statement came as a proposal was made in Congress that holders of the Army's Medical Corps valor badge be paid $10 more monthly. The bill was introduced by Represent. Bolton, R., Ohio.

However, Stimson said, recognition would have to be such that it would not impair the non-combat status of medics under the Geneva Convention, indicating it was not feasible to make them eligible for combat infantrymen's insignia and pay such as is extended to service forces personnel serving with combat units.

Stimson said the position of medics from the standpoint of pay was not unfavorable, because there is a larger proportion of technical ratings receiving higher pay in medical units than in order combat units.

While Allied medical personnel consisted mostly of males, two women helped with the injured at Bastogne. Augusta Chiwy, born in the Belgian colony of Congo, nursed patients throughout the war. In 2011, Chiwy, who was thought to have died in the war, was awarded the Order of the Crown from her country of Belgium and the Civilian Award for Humanitarian Service from the United States for her service. She died in 2015 at age 94.

Another Belgian nurse, Renée Bernadette Lemaire, was in Bastogne to visit her parents when the siege began. She volunteered to help the Allies and was working at a make-shift hospital set up in an abandoned store the night a bomb hit the hospital. Lemaire and a dozen or so others were killed.

Belgian nurse Renée Bernadette Lemaire is buried in Bastogne where she lost her life during the siege. Photo by author.

December 25, 1944

On the day when most American families were gathered around heavily-laden tables of food and opening gifts with loved ones, Allied troops were busy in the Ardennes:

- paratroopers of the 101st Airborne Division smashed several German attacks at Bastogne.

- Patton's counteroffensive south of Bastogne continued to encounter resistance by hard-fighting Germans.

- Allied lines held against strong enemy pressure directed due north in the Celles area against the Second Armored Division.

- Troops of the 26th Yankee Division remained embroiled in combat at Wiltz, Luxembourg.

After several hours, the weary troops of the 26th took refuge in a house not under direct fire. "I had to get away from the obnoxious sounds of nearly-frozen 155-millimeter cannon shells squealing like stuck pigs when leaving the barrels of divisional artillery," lamented Beresford Clarke.

Inside the shelter, Clarke bartered his prized Luger pistol for another soldier's worn-out tank driver jacket and overalls. Donning the dirty clothing over his wool pants and shirt, sweater, field jacket, long underwear,

underwear, and T-shirt, Clarke completed his winter apparel ensemble with a knitted ski mask from his mother.

STARS & STRIPES

Dear Santa Claus:

We have been good boys all this year and obey all orders given to us by our officers and non-coms.

When you come down our chimney will you please bring us each an overcoat.

Thank you Santa, and Merry Christmas to you.

Four Midgets

It had not taken Clarke and the other soldiers long to discover that at the Bulge a soldier's most prized garments were his items of clothing. Socks and boots were especially valued for keeping one's feet dry and clean. Continuously wet feet fell prey to painful ailments, including trench foot and frostbite, both of which could be severe enough for a soldier to be evacuated.

Ordinary combat boots were of little help in keeping feet warm in the subzero temperatures and deep snow. To fight against exposure troops stuffed their boots with straw and newspaper for insulation. Others carried spare pairs of heavy cotton socks under helmets to keep them dry when not in use.

Bob Heiny serves with the Ninth Armored Division.

Yet, even that amount of protection was not enough for many soldiers to avoid damage. "We lost more troops to frostbite and gangrenous feet than gun shots," said medic Bob Batchelder.

Robert Heiny, a soldier assigned to the Ninth Armored Division, must have seemed like Santa Claus as he distributed badly needed supplies to Allied soldiers. When the Fort Wayne, Indiana, native gave a new pair of boots to a soldier nestled in a foxhole, the soldier's face lit up. "He was so grateful!" said Heiny.

STARS & STRIPES

25 Dec. 1944

Driver Trades Boots with Obliging Major

T/Sgt. Lemuel C. Goodrich, of San Pedro, Calif., got a pair of combat boots for helping an engineer unit hurry through a new bridge.

Goodrich, with the 1055th Eng. Port Construction and Repair Gp., and other divers cleared debris at the site of a bridge blown up by the Germans.

The major in command of the engineer unit commended the divers and asked if there was anything he could do for them in return.

Said Goodrich, "I'd sure like a pair of boots like the ones you're wearing."

The major swapped footgear with the sergeant.

STARS & STRIPES   25 Dec. 1944

So That Others May Live By Harry J. McLaughlin WITH The 94TH INF. DIV., DEC 24

The small figure crawled forward, edged close to a hedgerow and started digging in. At his side was the telephone with which he was to observe the enemy's artillery fire and report back to his company. Suddenly the Jerries opened up with 88s and mortars. A piece of shrapnel hit him in the abdomen.

Gritting his teeth he called back to the CP: "Sarge, there is someone wounded up here. Send an aid man quickly."

Half an hour later he interrupted his observations to repeat: "Sarge, I'm dying, please hurry."

The aid man arrived but the observer refused to stop work while aid was being given. He was credited with neutralizing seven 88s and saving many lives. His own, though, could not be saved. The posthumous recommendation for the DSC for Pfc. Dale T. Proctor, of Bruno, Neb., reads: "He was a credit to his outfit and his country."

Franklin D. Roosevelt's Yule Message 1944

President Franklin D. Roosevelt sent Christmas greetings to men and women of the armed forces around the world:

"On behalf of a grateful nation, I send to the men and women of our armed forces everywhere warm and confident good wishes on this fourth Christmas of the war. On Christmas day we will remember you with pride and with humility, anguish and joy. We should keep remembering you all of the days of our lives."

President Franklin D. Roosevelt leads the United States into war.

Stars & Stripes

This Was America on Christmas Eve: Holiday Inspires Nation to Spur War Activity
by Joe Fleming, New York, December 25, 1944

Americans, fully aware the day would be grim for frontline doughboys, today awaited a Christmas dawn filled with deeper concern than probably any in history. But surging over this spirit of anxiety Americans quietly were expressing determination to provide every possible support from the home front.

Americans read Ike's order of the day and accepted it as a Christmas message far more potent than any they would ever again receive. In NY the Manpower Commission's regional labor committee put into a cable to Ike what most Americans were thinking:

"We feel your communique was a direct message to the home front as well, and so we accept it. We cannot match the sacrifice; we cannot equal the contribution the men on the battlefront are making under your gallant leadership, but we can and we do pledge to you and to them to rise to new heights of effort in bringing you the tools of war with which you are waging the fight."

Harold Bradley's journal:

Orders came down for us to attack at 0600 hours the next day. It would be my first time in combat. I was tank commander and didn't know what my reaction would be. It would turn out to be the darkest moment during my tour of duty.

When the time came, the ground was covered with ice. Our tanks slipped and slid all over the road, but we had our objective to take before night.

We had our plans worked out for the way to attack, but things didn't go so well. One of our tanks hit a mine. It was disabled and couldn't go any further. We advanced with our other four tanks for half a mile when one of our tank destroyers came up from a side road and pulled in front of our lead tank.

Jerry had that spot zeroed in. When the tank destroyer exploded, it trapped the rest of our tanks. We could not go forward.

We started to back our tanks up. When Jerry threw rounds at our tank in the rear, he could have trapped the rest of us. But we kept moving.

When the gunner of a German 88-mm gun started firing at my tank, I could see those shells plowing the earth over the side. Each shell seemed to get closer.

One covered me with dirt in the turret of my tank. I didn't know a tank could move so fast in reverse but finally my tank was under cover. We lost only one tank and tank destroyer that day. All I can say is it doesn't take long for a man to learn what it means to be scared. My Lord must have been riding with me.

Stars & Stripes

"Tiny Tree, With Tin Can Stars, Tells Joe It's Xmas"
by Jimmy Cannon

Long-leafed mistletoe hangs in snow-dusted clusters from the trees along the frozen road to the replacement center in this combat area. Firs taller than any Christmas trees these replacements had ever seen darken the slopes of the hills above the broken town.

And on Christmas Eve these rootless men of the army, who know lonesomeness more intimately than any other soldier, counterfeited a Yuletide spirit that was somber in its desperate ingenuity.

In the German barracks, where they wait for other men to die, they sat around a toy Christmas tree and a sad Santa Claus that Pvt. Robert C. Mastin, of Detroit, had modeled from mud and clay. (continued on next page) (cont'd) The muddy St. Nicholas was barrel-bellied and double-chinned, but his features were blurred and slack like an old prize fighter's. Santa's beard and cap were medical cotton and his cheeks were healthy with iodine from the dispensary. The snow on the little tree was flour sparkling with salt from the mess.

Stars cut and hammered from the tops of condensed milk cans testified by their perfection to Mastin's skill as a tool maker in civilian life. Tiny bulbs and electric light shades the Germans had left behind were painted whatever hues the supply sergeant had on hand.

But there were no gifts beneath the little tree with the milk can stars because these homeless men of the army hadn't received any mail for months.

"I got a wife, and a kid I've never seen," said Mastin. "I put the tree up for them. You know, to keep up the spirit. I couldn't get a present to send the kid on his first birthday."

A steady amount of snowfall during the next several days delayed and halted many tank advances. Still, the First Army pushed their way forward through snow-bound woods and fields, while the Third Army managed to beat off the final German troops around Bastogne.

An American Sherman tank sits on display in Bastogne where it operated against the Germans during the war. Photo by the author.

Near Celle, Belgium, a few miles from the Meuse River, the Second Armored Division with the help of Allied fighter-bombers knocked out 100 armored vehicles of the Germans' Second Panzer Division.

As Second Panzer survivors fled on foot, Patton's Fourth Armored Division broke through to Bastogne. This capped Patton's 4-day counterattack on the Bulge.

The tank battalion, led by Lt. Colonel Creighton Abrams, carved a corridor through which supply trucks and ambulances could reach the garrison. Allied airpower decimated German ranks, while Nazi armored units abandoned their weapons due to lack of fuel and ammunition.

**

In Hitler's headquarters in Berlin, General Alfred Jodl, Chief of the Armed Forces Operations Staff, and others of Hitler's military staff reviewed the results of nine days of fighting. It was obvious whatever lingering hopes the Germans had for success of an offensive was gone.

Their setbacks were massive. They had been slowed at St. Vith, trapped in the Ambleve River Valley, and frustrated at Bastogne. The objective of reaching the Meuse that should have been achieved by Day 2 now looked doubtful that it would ever happen.

The Germans had also been stopped at Elsenborn Ridge, though they had reduced by 5,000 the soldiers in the Second and 99th Infantry Divisions who were killed, wounded, or went missing.

When Jodl tried to convince Hitler that continuing to fight at the Meuse and pushing through to Antwerp was useless, Hitler finally agreed to fight east of the river, though he refused to give up on his objective of taking the Belgian port completely.

Having made his decision, Hitler then concentrated his attention on Bastogne. Earlier, when certain of advancing to Antwerp, Hitler had expressed little concern for taking the village. Now he saw Bastogne as a threat to the German line of communications. The village had to be under German command.

He immediately ordered German divisions from all parts of the Bulge to descend on Bastogne for a renewed siege on three sides.

Unfortunately for the German dictator, it was a failed re-attempt. When the Germans tried to cut off the neck of the salient into Bastogne, they were halted by the Americans who were by now strongly entrenched in the narrow corridor.

**

After weeks of constant combat, the 26th Yankee Division was pulled off of the front line 90 miles south of Bastogne. Assigned to R&R (rest and recreation), they headed for the recently liberated French village of Metz. There the troops found a coal mine shower facility for baths and Army barracks. "It was the first time we had been clean and slept in beds since going into action weeks earlier," said Beresford Clarke.

The break didn't last. Before daybreak, troops were awakened by non-commissioned officers distributing K rations, hand grenades, and bandoliers of ammunition for M1 rifles. After loading everything onto two-and-a-half-ton trucks, the 26th pulled out for Arlon, Belgium, 50 miles to the north.

**

In Luxembourg members of Patton's Third Army, 76th division, Company G, found the wintry conditions nearly impossible to navigate. Weeks of freezing temperatures with a lack of adequate food and clothing wore down even the most dedicated soldier.

When Company G was ordered to hike 28 miles to the front line, Dennis Butler, a front-line mortar gunner, tried to stay motivated, but it was difficult. "Most of the time it felt like for every step forward, we took one-half step back on snow and ice," he said.

Duane Wise fights at Normandy in summer of 1944.

Duane Wise with the 487th Anti-Aircraft Artillery Automatic Weapons Battalion had similar doubts about his survival.

In February 1944 the native of Albany, Indiana, had sailed with his unit to Liverpool, England. In June, they crossed the English Channel for the Battle of Normandy.

A few weeks later, Wise fought at Saint-Lô.

In the Ardennes, his unit were thrilled to find an empty barn. That night, they took refuge, falling asleep in the soft, aromatic hay as bombs fell around them.

By dawn, the shelling had stopped and the soldiers cautiously ventured outside. A surprise awaited them. On the ground a few feet from the barn lay an unexploded bomb. "If it had gone off, I would not have seen my 20th birthday," said Wise.

**

Having survived two near-death experiences, Private John Wearly of the 99th wondered if his luck would continue to hold. This became especially true when his next duty required all of his skill and courage.

As radioman for the platoon, Wearly was tasked with vacating his foxhole each night to examine the company's phone lines. "We didn't want them buried in the snow," he said. German snipers, land mines, and booby traps could all interfere with communiques to headquarters.

One night, while attending his duties with the phone lines, a shot flew past Wearly's right ear. Out of instinct, he fell in the snow. A soldier from his unit called out, inquiring about Wearly's status. When Wearly assured the soldier that he had not been hit, the soldier covered Wearly's movements with gunfire as he scurried safely back to safety.

**

Surrounded by constant combat and the grim reality of death, many soldiers looked for ways to alleviate stress.

Some troops smoked cigarettes and chewed gum distributed in ration kits. Alcohol, when it could be

Don LeMaster smokes a pipe to relieve stress on the battlefield.

found, was another popular means of lessening the mental strain of war.

First Army Quartermaster Don LeMaster didn't drink or smoke cigarettes. After chewing the gum in his ration kit, the Rome City, Indiana native searched for another way to relax.

One day, LeMaster spied a pipe in another soldier's mouth. Coming up with his own pipe, LeMaster happily stuck it in his mouth, unlit. At first, he appreciated how the wooden pipe stem gave his taut jaws something to gnaw on.

His relief and satisfaction were short-lived. "In one month, I had chewed the stem in half," he said.

**

Religion

Military chaplains hold church services between battles. Charles Dunwoody

Some soldiers turned to religion for help in dealing with the stress of war. Private Millard Schwartz read a New Testament Bible issued to soldiers by Gideons International before they disembarked from the States. He also sought God's help through prayer. "When we were behind cement pillboxes at the Siegfried Line, I asked God every day to let me live," he said.

In the many letters Robert Foster received from his wife, she mentioned God's faithfulness. "She reminded me of God's care through the difficult times of my life," he said.

Virgil Bixler saw many soldiers perish but felt God's protection around him. "I told myself nothing was impossible with God," he said.

**

Chaplains were an integral part of some military units. Pastors of the Protestant, Jewish and Catholic faiths volunteered for military service, performing a variety of duties -- conducting worship and memorial services, providing spiritual and moral guidance, working to boost morale, and assisting with grave registrations.

Tim Warner serves as assistant chaplain of the 95th Infantry Division at the Bulge.

Often, chaplains accompanied frontline units under fire, taking great personal risks while offering comfort to sick, wounded, and dying troops.

Timothy Warner of the 95th Infantry Division of the Third Army grew up attending a Methodist Church with his family in Davenport, Iowa.

After graduating from Davenport High School in 1943, Warner planned to enroll at seminary to become a preacher. Those plans were interrupted when he was drafted into the Army and sent for basic training to Fort Benning in Georgia. Later, Warner was sent to Army Specialized Training Program (ASTP). After the program closed, he was assigned to the 95th Infantry.

In September 1944, Warner's unit shipped from Boston to Liverpool, England, where troops bivouacked in tents in an apple orchard.

When Warner's interest in religion became known to his officers, he was assigned as assistant to Chaplain Homer Thompson, a Protestant pastor from Texas.

Some of Warner's duties included typing condolence letters to families of missing or dead soldiers (he had learned to type in high school). "I tried to personalize each letter with the name of the deceased," he said. "I was not allowed to provide details of how the soldier had died."

Warner also provided musical accompaniment for church services when no enemy troops were suspected in the area. He played on a portable pump organ which he and the chaplain hauled on a trailer they pulled with their jeep. Warner had taken piano lessons as a kid, but his musical repertoire was admittedly limited. "The most requested tune back home had been 'Here Comes the Bride' for weddings," he said. "There wasn't much demand for that on the battlefield."

Warner and Thompson drove a jeep painted with a red flag, indicating a chaplain was onboard. "Chaplains were to be afforded protection from the enemy," said Warner. "But that didn't always happen. More than once shrapnel from enemy fire went through our vehicle."

STARS & STRIPES

21 Dec. 1944
Life-Saving Gifts

A pocket Bible his mother gave him when he enlisted in the Army and a wallet his wife presented to him probably saved the life of Pvt. Richard K. Anderson, of Chinook Mont., and the 10th Armored Div. Anderson was carrying the gifts in his shirt pocket when an 88 shell exploded nearby. A fragment penetrated the wallet but was stopped by the Bible.

STARS & STRIPES

17 Dec. 1944

Runner Doubles as Jewish Chaplain

Six days a week, Pvt. Morris Lamb of Brooklyn, is a runner for H Company, 60th-Inf. Regt. On Saturday he puts on a prayer shawl and acts as chaplain for Jewish men of the regiment. He has been doing this since the divisional Jewish chaplain was killed during the battle of Mortain.

A Protestant chaplain delivers the sermon. Lamb, who attended Hebrew school in New York, conducts the prayer service.

Warner learned much from Thompson. "One night we drove through a section of the Bulge in a blackout," he said. "I could only see lights from the vehicle in front of us. That was a difficult situation, but he taught me patience."

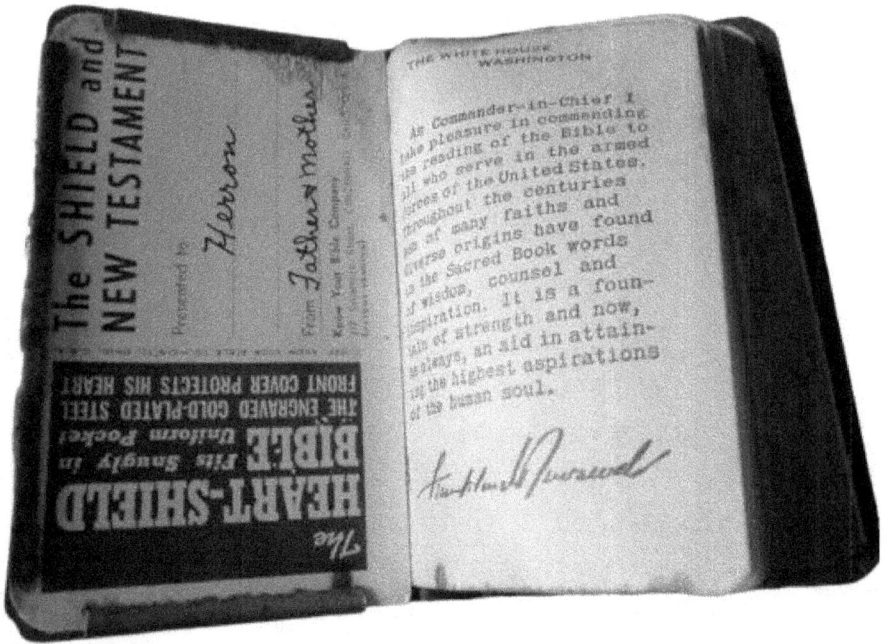

Many American troops receive a steel-plated New Testament with a message from President Franklin D. Roosevelt.

Harold Bradley's journal:

It was still snowing in Belgium and temperatures hovered between zero and 10 below. Our tanks had trouble staying on the road. Steel tracks on the tanks couldn't cut the mustard, so we fit them with rubber ones. Our maintenance officer had trouble finding the tracks but somehow, he came up with enough to outfit our battalion.

We accomplished our mission of destroying Task Force von Peiper. By doing this, we stopped the threat of a German penetration to Liege and the encirclement of Spa in Belgium.

For our work Company C was awarded a Presidential Citation.

**

As most infantry soldiers traveled on foot, it was rare for Theron Lindsey of the 75th Infantry Division to travel in a jeep. The one time the dairy farmer from Ossian, Indiana, hitched a ride, the vehicle passed over a land mine. The explosion threw Lindsey into the air, but thankfully, he was not injured.

Lindsey handled a rocket-propelled anti-tank weapon called a bazooka.

Troops and tanks make slow progress on icy roads in the Bulge. Beresford Clarke

When it was time to load the powerful weapon, Lindsey balanced it on his shoulder while another soldier inserted a rocket into the weapon's chamber from behind. A tap to the helmet alerted Lindsey when the job was completed. It was a deadly weapon and Lindsey never took for granted its killing power. "There was so much aggression on both sides," he said. "I saw friends killed. I was often scared."

That night, after German troops retreated over the crest of a hill, Lindsey wrapped himself in a blanket and sleeping bag before settling in the only safe spot he could find to sleep -- under a truck.

Chapter 8: Allied Gains
December 27-31, 1944

During the early days of fighting in the Bulge, the First Army endured heavy losses. Then two attack divisions were badly hit, forcing the Allies to face even more acute shortages in tanks and equipment. To procure enough rifles, ammunition, packs, and more for the battered divisions other units were ordered to turn in all excess equipment.

Old tanks with steel tracks, rather than rubber which was hard to obtain, were pressed into service. The change caused tricky maneuverability on icy roads.

From the north, south, and west American and British armies pressed in to squash German forces over snow-covered terrain in the Ardennes.

General Eisenhower, who was touring the fronts, sent a message to General Walter Bedell 'Beetle' Smith, his Chief of Staff: "Release to Omar Bradley at once the 11th Armored and 87th Divisions and organize a strong Bastogne-Houffalize attack."

As the Third Army widened its rescue corridor into Bastogne, the Germans gave ground. Patton's drive was led by the Fourth and Ninth Armored and 80th 'Blue Ridge' Infantry Divisions. Together, they pushed the Germans away from the supply road to Bastogne.

British Field Marshal Bernard Montgomery, commander of forces holding the Bulge's northern shoulder, didn't think the Allies were in a position to take control of the Ardennes. Believing the Germans had inflicted a disastrous defeat on the Americans, Montgomery proposed that the Allies should rest and reorganize for several months. Eisenhower vehemently disagreed. He ordered a reluctant Montgomery to launch a counteroffensive against the Germans west of the Rhine.

The rugged and reliable jeep fills vital roles in every theater of the war from front line reconnaissance vehicle to ambulance and VIP transport. Mark Flanagan.

STARS & STRIPES

28 Dec. 1944

Kids' Pennies Give Wounded in States Free Calls Home

WASHINGTON, Dec. 27 –

Wounded servicemen arriving here from overseas duty get free telephone service to their families in any part of the United States. Calls are paid for by the "First Call Home Fund," established by Washington Post from contributions from residents of the capital and surrounding area.

More than 13,000 has poured into the fund to enable wounded who have been back not longer than seven days to make calls from Walter Reed General Hospital and Bolling Field Hospital in Washington, and the Naval Medical Center at Bethesda, MD. For those whose families do not have phones, operators contact neighbors who are asked to pass on information that the serviceman is back. A garage operator in the Tennessee mountains recently drove 68 miles to get the wife of a soldier and bring her back to make the call to Walter Reed Hospital.

As Patton's Third Army crossed the German frontier to attack the Siegfried Line, it opened a second supply artery into the battered crossroads toward Bastogne.

Patton's drive was led by the 11th 'Thunderbolt' Armored and 87th 'Golden Acorn' Infantry, which jumped off in a swirling snowstorm. Their target was the crossroads at Houffalize, Belgium, 10 miles north of Bastogne. There the units ran into fierce resistance with von Manteuffel's Fifth Panzer Army.

The German attack was spearheaded by the elite First SS Panzer Division which tried to cut the supply line into Bastogne. The attack was defeated by the United States 35th 'Santa Fe' Infantry Division.

Von Manteuffel's Second Panzer Division attempted to continue its reach to the Meuse River, but was driven back by a combined force of the American Second Armored Division and British Third Royal Tank Regiment.

Three months earlier, Montgomery had tried to convince Eisenhower to invade Germany with a 'single thrust'. Again, Eisenhower paid no heed to the proposal and considered replacing the British officer.

**

As soldiers continued to suffer from exposure to frigid cold temperatures, an officer from the 95th Infantry asked the owners of a Belgian farmhouse for a place to sleep, perhaps in a barn. Daniel Frazier and the others were shocked at the farmer's response.

Not only did the farmer provide the soldiers with straw for sleeping and warmth, but offered food from his meager supplies.

Such actions, if discovered, would be considered acts of treason by the Nazis, punishable by death, not just of the farmer but his family. "It was a much-appreciated gift," said Frazier.

Another time the 95th was ordered to watch for enemy traffic on a nearby river. Upon discovering a barn overlooking the waterway, the soldiers stationed themselves near a window in the loft, then took turns sleeping and watching the river.

```
STARS & STRIPES

31 Dec. 1944

1945

The approach of New Year's
brought these expressions
yesterday: Prime Minister
Churchill: "We are entering upon
a year that should bring us
victory in Europe. Before many
months have passed the evil gang
who have too long dominated the
unhappy continent will be wiped
out."
```

Infantrymen of the 3rd Armored Division advance under artillery fire in a Belgian village.

On the cold, crisp morning, attack orders for Bastogne issued two days earlier by Eisenhower were carried out.

Troops of the 11th Armored and 87th Divisions moved to the offensive, joined by the 17th Airborne Division which had been held in reserve. The divisions crawled forward, their progress tediously slow. Towering snow drifts on icy roads made tank movements almost impossible.

The Germans unrelentingly attacked Bastogne, pounding away with their best divisions: infantry, paratroop, panzer. The conflict was intense as German power was thrown again and again in force against the Allies and citizens of Bastogne. Casualties soared, especially in the 101st Airborne and attached units.

The pressure continued for several days. Despite the fact that most of the soldiers were new to combat, the Allied salient into the town gradually widened. It became obvious they would be able to hold off the town's capture.

**

In a meeting at Hitler's headquarters, progress of the entire war was reviewed. The Germans were holding steady in fighting on the Italian and Eastern Fronts against the Soviet Army. While Hitler was confident his defenses along any front would halt any advance attempts, his aides acknowledged their failure to achieve objectives with the attack in the Ardennes.

But they felt they had prevented Allied penetration to the Rhine River. They were especially pleased with the information obtained of the transfer of airborne forces to the infantry as replacements. This, the Germans believed, would prevent for a while an airborne assault on the Rhine.

Hitler ordered Rundstedt to destroy the western Allies by a series of repeated blows, knocking them out, army by army.

The Germans' biggest concern was the shortages of labor and materials, especially fuel. Before an attack could be planned anywhere, it had to be determined if enough gasoline was available.

Chapter 9: Signs of Victory
January 1-7, 1945

Despite information of the transfer of Allied airborne forces to the infantry, Hitler, worried about air assaults on his ground troops and lines of communication, ordered the Luftwaffe into its last great attack of the war. Approximately 800-900 German planes blasted Allied air fields in Belgium and Holland, decimating 127 planes, mostly fighters, while damaging another 133. Allied retaliation was quick with possibly 200 German planes shot down or damaged.

A truck with injured Allied troops arrives at an aid station in Bastogne. Charles Dunwoody.

Hitler again directed Rundstedt to speed the capture of Bastogne with an attack from the southeast. But with Third Corps attackers squeezing the Germans into a pocket around Bastogne, it didn't allow the Germans sufficient maneuvering space to launch their own attack.

As the First Army began to press from the north, German General Model ordered an attack of panzer divisions from the north, northeast and the east. Hitler approved the plan.

However, it was painfully obvious to all that this coordinated attack on Bastogne would be the Germans' last. The Allies had reinforced its defenses along the Meuse River and the Third Corps was well entrenched at Bastogne with the 101st Airborne. With supporting armored and reinforcements from Patton, it appeared Hitler's plans to demolish Allied forces had failed.

**

Robert Walker, a farmer from Pennsylvania, witnessed evidence that the Nazi military was teetering on its last legs. While driving a jeep for supplies at the front, Walker more than once spotted German tanks and half-tracks abandoned along the road.

One day, he spied unfamiliar shapes under camouflage netting alongside of the road. Pulling over, he cautiously threw back the netting. Walker identified what he thought were engines. They were, in fact, Messerschmitt ME 262 jet engines -- the first ever built.

"Those powerful pieces just sat there abandoned, probably due to a lack of fuel," he said. "Under different conditions, they could have changed the course of the war. But without fuel they had no value."

Robert Walker delivers supplies to troops at the Bulge.

Harold Bradley's journal --

January 1:

My company received 12 new tanks. It took two days to get them to our staging area due to cold weather and snow that kept falling. Our next mission jumped off with A and B companies attached to the 325th glider Infantry Battalion of the 82nd Airborne Division.

**

January 3:

Company C remained in reserve. It was noisy as the 504th Parachute Infantry had a mission to take the high ground southeast of the village of Mont-de-Fosse, Belgium. Doing so would permit the 82nd Division to dominate all crossings of La Salm River in the vicinity of Grand Halleux.

By midnight, the 504th had done it. The quality of enemy forces was rapidly deteriorating. German SS troops were pulled out by von Rundstedt and less important troops put in. German air attacks had practically stopped.

**

January 7, 1945

Our company's next mission was to support the 508th Parachute Infantry south of the town of Arbrefontaine, Belgium. My platoon joined the Third Battalion of the 508th. During the attack, my tank crew destroyed an A.T. gun (antitank gun).

The next operation for us was on a line extending from the town of Malmedy, south to St. Vith. We were to drive to the northeast, pierce the Siegfried Line, and hold the position until relieved.

Reports came in that the Germans were beginning a counterattack north along the line leading from Herresbach, southeast of Malmedy. With our tanks and force of the 82nd we caught the German column by surprise, opening fire with all guns. Within minutes, we had killed 65 Germans and captured 200. No Americans were injured.

Our unit continued to endure through sleet and snow measuring three to four feet. We moved through small Belgian towns, receiving orders to drive to the Siegfried Line before the spring thaw. Along the way, we ran into small German fighting units whose motivation was nearly gone.

Messerschmitt ME 262 engines lay abandoned beside a road late in the war, possibly due to lack of fuel. Robert Walker.

January 8-25, 1945

With great reluctance, a by-now irascible Hitler was forced to admit that the cause in the Ardennes was lost. It was a bitter pill for the Fuhrer to swallow. His long-hoped-for dream of reaching the sea had vanished in the smoke of battle. The only consolation of the tremendous efforts of his troops involving a great cost of lives was that they had demolished the Allies' hopes of a quiet winter.

Hitler ordered the withdrawal of troops from the defensive line to west of the Bastogne-Houffalize Road. His only thought was to refit them to prepare for the coming Allied attack.

Both sides continued to suffer setbacks due to weather. Troops and tankers of the American First Army trudged toward Houffalize, a key crossroads a few miles north of Bastogne, though their progress was hampered by deep snowdrifts and continued sub-zero temperatures.

After riding overnight in a packed truck without blankets, troops with Company G arrived four miles west of Bastogne. "Jokes, smiles, and songs helped to keep our spirits up during hardships," said Dennis Butler.

He and the other soldiers set up camp in a clearing approximately 150 miles from the front. With temperatures below zero, a strong biting wind, and snow almost to their knees, Butler and his tent mate named Leo struggled to find firewood to warm themselves for the night.

"Our misery was hard to describe," said Butler. "The mess tent was 100 yards from our tent. By the time we made it back, my ration of peaches was frozen."

A soldier rests against a military vehicle settled in snow at the Bulge. Tim Warner.

As German troops retreated behind the Siegfried Line, Company G continued to march 18 miles through snow and over hills to overtake them. Upon approaching a large house that appeared to be abandoned, the Americans chose it as a place to bivouac.

The elegant home impressed the troops with its size and elegance. "It might have been a royal family's mansion," said Butler. The troops had their first bath in weeks in the Chateau – a nickname given to the structure by the Allies -- albeit from steel helmets.

They found a room large enough for the entire mortar section (approximately two dozen troops) to sleep. That night they assembled in the formation of canned sardines on the floor, grateful not to be on frozen ground as they had so many nights.

Troops from Company G bivouac in an elegant abandoned home. Dennis Butler.

**

Trekking through Europe, Virgil Bixler and members of the 905th Field Artillery helped to capture three significant objectives. One was a group of 5,000 German soldiers, including several top-ranking officials and SS troops.

The second seizure was 29 train cars of Benzene. The chemical warfare agent had been used with deadly effects by the German military against their enemies in WWI. "I hate to think what that could have done to our troops," said Bixler.

His unit scored yet another prize -- an enormous German gun requiring two railroad cars for transportation.

The weapon, which Allied troops nicknamed 'Big Bertha', could fire seven miles. It had been kept hidden in a mountain under armed guard.

American troops discover an over-sized German gun hidden in a mountain. Beresford Clarke.

The Bulge took a smoother shape as the Third Army and a British division met at St. Hubert, 15 miles west of Bastogne. British troops also claimed a victory upon retaking La Roche, a village northwest of Bastogne.

The United States V Corps cut into the German flank further to the east. More than 800 of Hitler's tanks and the last of the Third Reich's fighter aircraft were destroyed.

Tankers of the American First and Third Armies finally linked up in Houffalize, a key crossroads in the Ardennes. When their converging attacks forced the Germans to abandon the post, the once-threatening 60-mile Bulge was flattened to a 15-mile bump.

In spring 1945 German troops, many of them youths, surrender to the Allies. Dennis Butler.

As First and Third armies continued their drives toward Houffalize, German units retreated from the area, scurrying back toward Berlin. The Americans wheeled to the east to start operations toward the West Wall.

The Seventh Armored Division crashed through the German crust into St. Vith from where they had been driven a month earlier. They continued to struggle against deadly weather as much as tough German resistance.

A convoy of soldiers from the Soviet Union marches west toward Nazi headquarters in Berlin. Charles Dunwoody

Patton's 26th 'Yankee' Infantry division took Wiltz, Luxembourg and the Third Army continued to regain lost ground as it advanced over the Clerf River to march toward the Belgium-Germany border. The German military offered little defense, having lost all of their tanks and nearly all of their Luftwaffe aircraft.

The Wehrmacht made a full retreat, relocating the front lines back to where they were before the attack on December 16. For all practical purposes, the war in the west involving the raging battle that was to be the greatest German offensive ever was over.

The reality of a likely German defeat finally penetrated Hitler's addled mind. Giving up his last major offensive of the war, he left his Western Front command post near Frankfort-on-Main, returning to his underground bunker in Berlin where he would spend the last 105 days of his life before ending it on April 30, 1945 by gun shot.

On May 8, 1945 – a date that would become known as 'VE Day' or 'Victory in Europe Day' -- German military officials signed terms of unconditional surrender to the Allies in Reims, France.

Six and a half years after Hitler invaded Poland, the war in Europe was over!

**

Sadly, another world leader would not live to celebrate the end of the long war.

In January 1945, President Roosevelt had sailed from Newport News, Virginia, to the island nation of Malta near Africa and Italy where he planned to meet with British Prime Minister Winston Churchill. The purpose of this conference and another the pair would have with Stalin a few weeks later at Yalta in the Soviet Union would be to discuss post-war plans.

For several months Roosevelt had showed signs of increasing ill health. The strain of the war exacerbated his condition, causing him -- the only American president to be elected to four consecutive terms of office – to die on April 12, 1945, from a cerebral hemorrhage at his home in Warm Springs, Georgia.

On that same day, Vice President Harry S. Truman was sworn in as President of the United States. Most Americans knew little, if anything, about the new leader from Missouri who was now in charge of the war. They hoped he could lead them to victory.

Truman's decision to drop atomic bombs on the Japanese cities of Hiroshima (August 6, 1945) and Nagasaki (August, 1945) did just that by forcing Japanese Emperor Hirohito to announce his country's surrender on August 15, 1945. The formal surrender agreement was signed on September 2, 1945, aboard the U.S. battleship USS *Missouri*, anchored in Tokyo Bay.

**

More than million Allied troops, including 500,000 Americans, fought in the Battle of the Bulge. Approximately 19,000 soldiers were killed in action with 47,500 wounded and 23,000 missing in action. An estimated 100,000 Germans were killed, wounded or captured.

During the Battle of the Bulge, U.S. forces did not have the benefit of prepared defenses. They suffered heavy bombing, intense artillery fire, and constant infantry and armor attacks on all sides of their cut-off and encircled positions, all the while contending with dwindling supplies and injuries.

Clerks, cooks, mechanics, drivers, and others manned the front line, though they were vastly outnumbered. All did their duty with a "do or die" attitude of commitment and sacrifice, functioning for days with little sleep or food.

They stopped every German attack, allowing time for others to arrive and lift the siege of Bastogne, and to save much of Luxembourg from another German invasion.

But the really significant outcome of the Battle of the Bulge was that it very likely saved the Allies a great many more casualties. If the Germans had used their quarter of a million men lost in the Battle of the Bulge to fortify and protect Germany, Allied losses for the remainder of the war would likely have been much greater.

Chapter 10: After the War

The return of American military personnel began with dozens of voyages of crowded ships across the Atlantic. But it would require several months before all men and women were granted the opportunity to go home.

Corporal Gene Valentine continued to work in medical aid stations, although he and other military personnel happily saw a decrease in their number of patients. "We could relax a little and play basketball when off-duty," he said.

When his hospital moved to Antwerp, Belgium, Valentine was transferred to an amphibious engineer unit in Southampton, England. He was there upon receiving his discharge in January 1946.

**

Ray Boyer's and others in the CCR of the Ninth Armored Division were awarded the Presidential Unit Citation for collective combat heroism, having scored a victory that permitted other units to rally and set up positions to defend Bastogne. The CCR was also awarded the Belgian Croix de Guerre with Palm for bravery and military virtue on the battlefield.

**

By the war's end, the *Queen Mary* had made 31 voyages, transporting 380,000 ground fighting troops to the European Theater of Operations. It was a small wonder that Hitler had put a high price on the ship's sinking. The

City of Long Beach, California purchased the ship, permanently docking it there where it serves as a hotel.

**

In December 2020, the American Battle Monuments Commission (ABMC) officially accepted the Battle of the Bulge Monument as their 31st Federal Monument. Known previously as the Mardasson Memorial, the monument stands as a tribute of the Belgian people to the American soldiers who died during the Battle of the Bulge. The

The Battle of the Bulge Monument in Bastogne commemorates American soldiers who gave their lives for the Belgian people. Photo by author.

Battle of the Bulge Monument is the sole memorial commemorating all American forces who fought during the Battle of the Bulge.

Chapter 11: Back Home

Vernon Affolder returned to his home in Decatur, Indiana and worked in the insurance business.

**

Andy Anderson worked in Indianapolis for Indiana Bell. He married and became a father to four children.

**

Bob Batchelder sold wholesale food products in Fort Wayne. He married and was the father of one son.

**

Virgil Bixler worked at Central Soya in Decatur, Indiana. He and Garnett became parents to three children.

**

Ray Boyer and his wife, Fleta, lived with their three children in Alexandria, Virginia, where he worked as a meat cutter. He attended military reunions and was a member of the Veterans of the Battle of the Bulge.

**

Harold Bradley received a Bronze Battle Star and Silver Star for heroism and a Purple Heart for an injury. He worked at the Pauls Valley Daily Democrat for 37 years before retiring in 1986. In 1999, members of the 740th Tank Battalion and citizens of Dalhem / Neufchateau and surrounding areas dedicated a monument to members of his battalion. In July 2004 Bradley returned to Europe to view areas where he and others from his unit had fought.

**

Dennis Butler and his wife became parents to two sons. He sold insurance.

**

Beresford Clarke finished his degree from Purdue University as a mechanical engineer. He married and fathered three children.

**

Charles Dunwoody served as a chaplain's assistant in the 83rd Army. After the war, he farmed in Ohio, married and became a minister in his church.

**

Mark Flanagan used the GI bill to pay for courses at Miami University. He worked for Procter and Gamble, Central Soya, and Fort Wayne National Bank.

**

Bob Foster worked for the U.S. Postal Service and a fire department in Fort Wayne. He and Phyllis were married for 71 years and parented two children.

**

Daniel Frazier married and became a father to four sons. He worked as a pipe fitter journeyman.

Bob Heiny ran an advertising business and coached basketball in Fort Wayne. He was married and the father of three daughters.

**

Don LeMaster married and was the father of two sons. In 1985 he returned to Europe where residents thanked him for his service during World War II.

**

Theron Lindsey graduated from Indiana Technical College with a civil engineering degree. He worked for the state highway department.

**

Keith McComb served as a photographer with the Eighth Air Force. He married and raised a family in Fort Wayne, Indiana.

**

Millard Schwartz and his wife became parents to two sons. In 2012 he was awarded an honorary Master's Degree in Military Arts from Cumberland University for time served with the Tennessee Maneuvers.

**

Don Shady worked at Central Soya in Decatur, Indiana. He attended military reunions for the 435th Squadron Group.

**

Bob Staggs drove a truck for the Coca-Cola Company in Muncie. He and his wife became parents to two sons.

**

Gene Valentine drove trucks for Fruehauf Trailers in Fort Wayne. He married and became the parent of one son.
**

Bob Walker worked as an engineer at S.F. Bowser, Inc. He and his wife became parents to three children.

**

Tim Warner earned his doctorate and became president of Fort Wayne Bible College from 1970-1980.

**

John Wearly taught school and became a director of Boy Scouts. In 1995, he attended the 50th anniversary of America's involvement in World War II in Europe.

**

Max Whiteleather worked on the railroad for many years. He and his wife were parents to three children. He attended military reunions.

**

Dick Willey married and became the father of four daughters. He worked for Franklin Electric in Bluffton.

**

Duane Wise owned grocery stores in Muncie. He married and he and his wife became the parents of two children.

Book Club Questions

1. Leaders of the Allies were criticized for being caught unaware of the December 16th invasion. Based on examples given in the book of the Germans' preparatory moves, do you think this was fair?
2. When John Wearly became separated from his unit and had to evade capture, he thought of his family. What thoughts have gone through your head when you faced a stress-filled situation?
3. Several veterans discuss seeking refuge in foxholes in the cold weather and fighting. What have you used as a method of safety or retreat in your life?
4. Adolf Hitler continued to believe he could gain control of the war in the Ardennes despite a dearth of soldiers and supplies. Based on reasons explained in the book, were his generals right in trying to convince him to drop the plans?
5. Medics at the Bulge put their lives at risk on the front lines. Have you ever helped someone in the midst of danger? Explain.
6. The battle for Bastogne caused many deaths. Should General Anthony McAuliffe have surrendered his forces rather than continue to fight it out?
7. Soldiers in the book discovered abandoned vehicles and weapons by the enemy, due to lack of fuel and parts. How might the battle in the Bulge have been different if the Germans had unlimited resources?

8. Many soldiers returned from the war reluctant to talk about the Bulge and other battles. Why do you think they kept their stories to themselves?
9. Winston Churchill was quoted as saying he believed the Battle of the Bulge was one of the world's greatest battles. Do you agree?
10. Which story or incident from the book impacted you the most? Why?

Read an exciting excerpt from Kayleen Reusser's book, *Captured! Stories of American WWII Prisoners of War:*

A single dim light illuminated the hold of the ship where 1,800 men stood crushed together. A few among the tired bodies raised their heads, desperately gasping for a breath of fresh air of which there was none in the fetid compartment. The only good thing about being packed tightly was they could hold each other up, while allowing some prisoners a chance to sit.

As the Russian army had begun making their way west in the latter part of World War II, German guards and officials at Stalag VI, a prisoner of war camp in the northernmost confines of the German Reich (what is today Lithuania), had received orders to move their prisoners.

In early 1945, the large group of weak and often ill men had boarded a decrepit sea craft at the port of Memel on the Baltic coast. During the sea journey which took days the prisoners suffered dehydration, starvation, and dysentery.

As the miserable journey continued, some men began to fret about its destination. For 18-year-old Walter Rumple, radio operator on a B-17 before it was shot down, it didn't matter where the ship docked. He was determined to survive any hell the Germans put him through.

**

World War II Timeline

1933

Adolf Hitler is appointed chancellor of Germany; the first of hundreds of killing centers over Europe is established at the German village of Dachau.

1938

Germany invades Austria; Hitler holds his last annual rally in Nuremberg, which draws one million people who support his practices and ideals.

1939

Hitler invades Poland and Czechoslovakia, causing both countries to surrender; Nazis begin persecuting Polish Jews; the United States sells military supplies to Britain and France to support their efforts to oppose the Nazis; Great Britain, Australia, New Zealand, Canada, South Africa and India declare war on Germany in fall, making this the official start to World War II.

1940

Germany takes over Denmark, Norway, Belgium, Netherlands, Luxembourg, and France; Winston Churchill becomes Britain's new Prime Minister; Italy joins the war with Germany; the Battle of Britain begins when Germany bombs London and other British cities -- the 'Blitz' on London continues for 57 nights, killing more than 40,000 citizens; Japan joins Italy and Germany in fighting the Allies; American president Roosevelt is elected to a third term, the only time an American president will serve more than two terms; Roosevelt bans racial discrimination in war-industry employment.

1941

Germany invades Greece; the United States continues to send military equipment and other supplies to the Allies with payment deferred until after the war; Germany attacks the Soviet Union; the Soviet Union joins the Allies; Japan attacks Pearl Harbor, along with other Allied bases in the Pacific and Asia, the result being the United States and Great Britain declare war on Japan; Germany and Italy declare war on the United States.

1942

The Nazis establish a plan to kill European Jews via death camps; Japanese troops take control of large portions of East Asia and the Pacific, including Hong Kong, Singapore, the Philippines, Thailand, Malaysia and Burma; United States invades North Africa; United States wins the Battle of Midway, a major turning point in the war in the Pacific; people of Japanese heritage are interned in the United States.

1943

Italy is invaded by the Allies and surrenders; Mussolini is removed from power; Italy begins secret peace talks with the Allies and eventually declares war on Germany; Allied leaders meet to discuss Operation Overlord, the Allied invasion of Normandy, France, against Germany's armed forces.

1944

In January General Dwight D. Eisenhower takes charge of planning Operation Overlord, which takes place in June; Allies push German forces toward Germany, liberating many cities including Paris; Roosevelt is elected to his fourth term as United States president; in December, the Germans attempt a last-ditch effort to overcome the Allies by splitting their troops, a strategy that becomes known as the Battle of the Bulge; Allied island-hopping in the Pacific liberates the Philippines.

1945

Prisoners at Dachau and dozens of other death camps throughout Europe are freed; Allies defeat the Germans in the Battle of the Bulge; Allies take the Pacific island of Iwo Jima; Churchill, Roosevelt and Stalin meet for the last time in Yalta to discuss the end of the war and how to divide Germany; in April Roosevelt dies and Vice President Harry S. Truman is sworn in as president;

Mussolini is captured and executed by his own people; Hitler commits suicide in his underground bunker in Berlin; Germany surrenders in May; Truman declares the end of the European war on May 8 as V-E Day (Victory in Europe); United States drops atomic bombs on the Japanese cities of Hiroshima and Nagasaki; the Soviet Union declares war on Japan; Japan's Emperor Hirohito accepts the Allies' terms of surrender on August 14, which becomes known as V-J Day (Victory over Japan); American troops begin returning home, while others are assigned to Japan and Europe during the Allied period of occupation.

1946

Joachim Peiper and dozens of German soldiers accused of committing various murders are caught and sentenced to death during war trials held at Dachau. Many are released after serving 12 years of imprisonment. In 1976 Peiper is found murdered in his home in France. His assassin is never caught.

A stone memorial honoring the 84 Americans killed at Malmedy stands across the field where the murders occurred. Local citizens maintain the site, which includes the engraved names of the soldiers and fresh flowers planted in their memory.

Glossary

besieged: Crowded in upon; surrounded.

cadre: A group of officers and enlisted personnel necessary to establish and train a new military unit.

casualty: Soldier who is killed, injured, captured, or missing in action after a battle.

counterattack: Assault by a ground combat unit to drive back an enemy.

decimate: To destroy a great number of something.

garrison: A body of troops stationed in a fortified place.

gas mask: Breathing device worn to cover the nose, mouth, and eyes to give protection from a gas attack.

infantry: American military division of thousands of troops divided into regiments and battalions. They form the backbone of attack and defense forces.

invade: To enter a place, such as a country, with the aim of taking control of it.

Jerry: A nickname used by Allies for German troops.

land mine: Explosive charge concealed under the surface of the ground or road, designed to be detonated by pressure or proximity of a vehicle such as a tank or a person.

panzer: Vehicle, usually tank, making up the German military.

rations: Fixed portions of food or goods usually considered necessary for survival.

regime: Government in power.

sabotage: Treacherous action, such as the destruction of property, to defeat or hinder a cause.

salient: Central outward-projecting angle of a projection in a battle line.

siege: Act of surrounding and attacking a fortified place to isolate it from help and supplies in order to lessen resistance of the defenders and promote surrender.

squadron: Military unit.

synchronize: Cause to move at the same exact rate and pattern.

tactical: Maneuver or plan of action designed to gain a desired end or advantage.

Index

About the Author

Kayleen Reusser's books are available on Amazon. She appreciates reviews posted there and at Goodreads. Reusser is the wife and mother of Air Force airmen, as well as two daughters. She presents in-person and virtual talks about WWII.

www.KayleenReusser.com

We Fought to Win: American WWII Veterans Share Their Stories (Volume 1, World War II Legacies)

They Did It for Honor: Stories of American WWII Veterans (Volume 2, World War II Legacies)

We Gave Our Best: American WWII Veterans Tell Their Stories (Volume 3, World War II Legacies)

We Defended Freedom: Adventures of WWII Veterans (Volume 4, World War II Legacies)

D-Day: Soldiers, Sailors and Airmen Tell about Normandy (Volume 1, World War II Insider)

Battle of the Bulge: Stories From Those Who Fought and Survived (Volume 2, World War II Insider)

Captured! Stories of American WWII Prisoners of War

Women of WWII Coloring Book

It Was Our War Too: Youth in the Shadows of WWII